Glory H

By
Brian Darling

Brian Darling

Best wishes

you Macti

ISBN: 978-0-244-31709-6

PublishNation
www.publishnation.co.uk

For my wife Sinead and for Dan, Tom, Sarah and Aidan. Also for my brother John, who took me to my first ever match.

The Macari Centre
Street Retreat

Registered Charity Number

1168463

The Macari Centre was established by the Macari Foundation in 2016 and offers direct access accommodation for people who are sleeping rough on the streets of Stoke on Trent. The centre offers warmth, safety and shelter to those who find themselves sleeping rough, offering hospitality and care and reducing poverty for some of the most vulnerable people in our society. We provide food and a bed with the help and support from a dedicated team of Staff and Volunteers we work with other agencies in the city to give our customers the help they need to support them into more sustainable accommodation and move forward accessing the services they need to bring change to their lives.

CHAPTER ONE
Introduction

I am going to deal with this *Why Glory Hunter* thing in a minute, but first let me tell you what this book is really about.

I am a proud Stoke City fan and have been over five decades. It feels like its always been an important part of my life and I have built relationships with family, friends, colleagues and acquaintances all around my passion for red and white stripes. This book is as much about those relationships, with my dad, my older brother and eventually with my sons and how I use Stoke City as really important glue.

The world has changed since I started attending Stoke City matches in 1976. Concorde's first commercial flight took off in January of that year. Harold Wilson resigned as Prime Minister in March and was superseded by James Callaghan. Apple Computer Company was formed by Steve Jobs and Steve Wozniak. The Sex Pistols performed the first of two concerts to an audience of 40 people in Manchester's Lesser Free Trade Hall – where members of the audience went on to form the groups Joy Division, New Order, The Smiths, Simply Red and The Buzzcocks. The Eagles released their album *Hotel California* (I still listen to my copy), Shay Given was born, and the highest grossing film was Rocky, the first one.

This book is for dads who take their sons to the match. For men who still go to the game with their dad. For friends across many decades and continents who remain connected because of their sporting passions. For me it was Stoke City, for many others it is a different club and for even more people it will be a different sport

1

that provides the adhesive.

As I track my experiences over the last 40 plus years, spanning five decades, some things don't seem to have changed at all. The way I feel and anticipate the match day experience for example. I think that's a good thing and while everything else in my life has been changing, Stoke City is a constant; regardless of who the players have been through different eras. In this book I use my working life in banking to chart the progress of my team and reflect on how Stoke City provide a strange kind of balance to economic turmoil. Many who know me from work will reach out to these parts of the book.

Back to Glory Hunter, I promised to explain this. Just about everyone, without exception says it, "Glory Hunter? But you're a Stoke fan?" Admit it, you've been thinking it too, wondering how on earth this could possibly apply to Stoke City. This is my explanation.

In the early 1970's Stoke were actually bloody good. They won the (League) Cup and challenged for the First Division title (now the Premier League). They were horrendously unlucky in successive FA Cup semi-finals against Arsenal - my Dads team - and were playing European football against the likes of Ajax. So you see, I am a Glory Hunter!

The reality of course is that through the combination of Stoke being quite successful for a relatively short period, the advice of a mate at primary school and the appeal of a red and white striped home team strip, meant that I would commit to a life time season ticket with this giant of the First Division. This was also the team boasting the best goalkeeper in the world - Gordon Banks.

It seemed a good deal to me, what could possibly go wrong? At my school I was out on a limb and surrounded by Liverpool and

Manchester United fans. I was happy though, Stoke were playing well and I took my passion into senior school – unlike many others who would flit from team to team depending on latest results.

Little did I know of the pain, love, hopelessness, jealousy, disappointment and sheer despair to come. Take the 2017 FA Cup 3rd Round tie against Wolves for example, where we lost at home 0 – 2 to this lower league Staffordshire rival in an abject performance. Then just occasionally, the unbridled joy and ecstasy of narrow triumph. In fact it doesn't even need to be a victory, sometimes a draw is plenty good enough.

All these emotions create the narrative of my football-supporting career. Career? Is it a job? Well it certainly feels like it sometimes, travelling to Wigan in midweek to watch your team lose 6 - 1 is hard work. Or Hartlepool away on a winter Saturday (more about that experience later).

I don't know if it's an age thing but I have discovered that, whatever the situation, despite how dire the last performance might have been, there is a relatively short healing period.

For example, I mentioned the Wolves game. Stoke City are an established Premier League club, having finished 9th and in the top half of this massively competitive league for the past three years. Wolves are a Championship side who, at the time of writing, were struggling in sixteenth place in their league (one league below the Premier League and a world of difference in terms of financial rewards and hence ability to entice the best players). They had lost seven of their last fifteen games, winning just three times and keeping a clean sheet on just three occasions. So, Wolves visit Stoke on Trent, win fairly comfortably 2 – 0 (a 4/1 bet at Bet365) and leave the home faithful shaking their heads and questioning the entire future of their club.

3

Within a matter of days, after time for adequate mourning, I am restored to full fitness and belief, ready and eagerly anticipating our next game following the Wolves debacle. The next game is away at Sunderland, whom we had not beaten in the league at their stadia for twenty-three years. I use the term stadia as Sunderland relocated to the purpose built Stadium of Light in 1997, prior to which they occupied Roker Park, where we last won in 1994. The Stadium of Light is one of my favourite stadium designs, its big (the capacity of 49,000 is the eighth largest of any English football stadium) and unusually for pretty much off the shelf pop up football stadia, has character. As the players are about to enter the arena they play Prokofiev's highly distinctive Dance of the Knights. If you don't recognise it from being at the stadium, you will probably have heard it on The Apprentice. It's played very loudly and makes the hairs on the back of my neck stand up.

So just a few days after embarrassing defeat we are getting ready to go again, at a ground we have failed to win at in the league for nearly a quarter of a century. Its irrational I know and it's akin to how Superman responds to a heavy beating. He's seemingly down and out, then the next minute up and ready for the fight again.

These emotions and the rollercoaster ride that is a Stoke City fans world, have punctuated my life (and maybe yours too). Most of what follows has a football bias, my football bias. It's only my personal perspective and experience, which many people might think and feel differently about.

It's been an emotional journey, a journey that only ends when I do, but if it wasn't emotional, what would it be worth?

By the way, we beat Sunderland 3 – 1.

4

CHAPTER TWO
How it all started

My home between the age of 5 until my mid-twenties was in Rugby. My Dad had got a job at *English Electric* and for most of this period we lived at number 7 St Anne's Road. It was one of the more attractive roads of Council Houses in Overslade, Rugby and was a generous traditional three bed roomed semi. Further down the road, towards its end over a hill and on the left was Hudson Road. This was also a part of the same council estate. The type of housing in Hudson Road and a number of other local roads was a less traditional construction. It consisted of British Iron and Steel Federation (BISF) houses with steel trussed sheeting as the outside cladding on the upper storey. These were functional but unattractive houses and locally known as *Tin Town*.

BISF housing was erected from 1946. The design sponsored by BISF could be erected much faster than traditional housing and was used to replace the many thousands of houses destroyed in bombings during WWII.

They looked horrible.

In one of the first houses on the left in Hudson Road, number 5 I think, lived Gary Devine with his family including two older brothers. Gary wasn't a big lad, but tough and wiry, easily much harder than me. He wasn't everyone's cup of tea at school, but was my pal and followed West Brom. To this day I have no idea why. I didn't question it at all. If Gary was a West Brom fan he would have a good reason for it. They had won the League Cup in 1966 and followed this up with an FA Cup Final victory in 1968, when they beat Everton in extra time thanks to a single goal from Jeff Astle. Perhaps Gary was a Glory Hunter too?

Anyway, Gary was good at football, much better than me, tougher in the tackle and a tricky dribbler with a powerful shot. I remember he complimented me once saying that I was *"as good as he was this time last year"*. I know it was meant with good intent as a compliment and I was happy with that. What it really meant however was that he was pretty good and I was pretty crap. We played in the park, in the school playground and anywhere that we found space to kick a ball.

When it came to learning about football, I listened to Gary and he told me that Stoke City had the best defence in the league. At the time this was the First Division – today's Premier League, so probably best in the world as well. At its heart was Gordon Banks, England's famous 1966 World Cup winner and the goalkeeper responsible for the miraculous save from Pele in the 1970 World Cup Finals in Mexico, still described by many as the greatest save in the history of the game.

Gordon Banks (OBE) won 73 caps for England and is widely regarded as one of the greatest goalkeepers of all time. He was Footballer of the Year in 1972 (when we won the League Cup) and named FIFA Goalkeeper of the Year on six occasions. He is a legend of the game. But for injuries sustained in a terrible car crash on 22nd October 1972, travelling home after a session with the Stoke physiotherapist on an injured shoulder, he would have enjoyed many more appearances both in an England and Stoke City shirt.

His car, a Ford Consul (a re-badged Ford Granada Mk 1) collided with an oncoming Austin A60 Van and ended up in a ditch. After surgery at North Staffordshire Hospital, during which he received 200 stitches to his face and more than 100 micro-stitches inside the socket of his right eye, his sight never returned in that eye. He retired from professional football the following Summer. I was stunned by this.

At the 1970 World Cup finals in Mexico, England had progressed to the Quarter Finals stage where they would meet West Germany, losing finalists in 1966. Gordon was absent due to a suspicious stomach illness, where the day before the game he was affected by violent stomach cramps. He was replaced by Peter Bonetti, who had a single England Cap under his belt. England were beaten 3 – 2.

My belief is that we would have won that game and the World Cup tournament had it not been for Peter Bonetti (this was the first World Cup finals where I had taken a real interest and where I was able to watch on TV, as in 1966 I was only 5 years old). We were cruising at 2 - 0 well into the second half and until Norman Hunter, a rugged no nonsense defender tried some Lionel Messi type skills on the touch line. He lost the ball and Germany scored from the attack that followed. That's ok, I thought, we're still winning; but not for long. I blamed Bonetti and felt that his goalkeeping had cost us dearly, mistakes I felt that Banksy would never have made.

I met Peter at a Chelsea v Stoke FA Cup Quarter Final in 2010 as he popped into the box I had been invited to. He was a very charming man and great with all the guests. I was tactful enough not to remind him of the game in Mexico, and even though I thought he was a nice bloke - it didn't mean I forgave him.

So, after all that, it was a no brainer, I am now a Stoke City fan. Gordon Banks and all!

I hadn't realized at the time that Rugby was 75 miles from Stoke on Trent. I hadn't a clue how to get there or precisely where it was. I knew that it was a Midlands based club because I discovered that my team were regulars on *Star Soccer*, a weekly football highlights program featured on ATV (Associated TeleVision) between 1965 and 1983, when it was replaced by a networked *The Big Match*. ATV was a Midlands only broadcaster and the program was hosted initially by Billy Wright and then Gary Newbon. The main commentator was the distinctive Hugh Johns (who was also ITV's man at the microphone for the 1966 FIFA World Cup Final).

This show featured extended highlights of a Midlands based match and then shorter highlights of two other games from around the country, usually involving Midlands teams.

The program was broadcast during a glory period for a number of Midlands based teams. Derby County, Nottingham Forest and Aston Villa all won First Division League championships (the latter two also adding European Cups). Wolverhampton Wanderers won the League Cup twice, a feat that the mighty Potters also achieved in 1972.

I am not sure if Gary had been watching Stoke on Star Soccer or whether this was the source of his interest in West Brom, but it was a great find and was my main source of viewing for my team.

Gary and I grew apart as we went to different senior schools. He went to The Herbert Kay and I went to the more local Harris Church of England High School. I rarely saw him again and regretted the one occasion when I was riding my bike back from a mates house when I recognised him and yelled 7 - 0 loudly as I passed him at speed!

No, Stoke hadn't beaten West Brom 7 - 0, it was in fact Ipswich Town who had delivered this thumping in 1976, which remains a record league victory in their 138 year history. Interestingly Stoke's record League win is against West Brom, 10 – 3 in fact, but unfortunately this was in 1937 and the nearest goal glut I have

8

witnessed between the two clubs was a 6 – 0 mauling at the Hawthorns. I had the displeasure to attend with a few workmates from Birmingham who were West Brom fans. Don Goodman got a couple that day.

The regret I felt at calling out to Gary wasn't a case of humility catching up with me, it still rarely does even now. It was that I knew if he ever caught up with me, I would be "dead meat". Fortunately for me, he never did.

Stoke City - Cup Winners

Winning the League Cup in 1972 didn't just dry the ink on my lifetime contract with the club, it made it indelible. I was nearly 11, Gary was obviously right with his astute observations about our defence and we were cup winners against Chelsea. I had followed my clubs progress but nowhere near as closely as it's possible to do these days. I never quite realised the drama that unfolded in the series of games with West Ham in the Semi Final stage.

I was proud to learn that, in one of those games Banksy again proved his world class status with a worldie of a save against a Geoff Hurst penalty, a fellow 1966 World Cup winner. Banksy regards this save a better one than his save against Pele in 1970.

I mentioned that keeping in touch wasn't so easy in those days. Long before Internet, mobile phones or live televised matches and with the signal for Radio Stoke being very fragile at best when trying to pick this up 75 miles away in my bedroom in Rugby. Coverage came at the end of either the BBC or ITV news. It was hellishly infuriating and occasionally I resorted to phoning the ground in the hope that someone would answer and I could ask them the score. I remember doing this with about 10 minutes left in the FA Cup game against Blyth Spartans. After several rings a fairly irritated person

9

answered the phone and told me the score was 2 - 1. I was really pissed off, only winning 2 - 1 against this non league outfit, after we had comprehensively dispatched Tilbury 4 - 0 in round 3, a game I attended and enjoyed from the heart of the Boothen End.

I was wrong to be disappointed at 2 - 1 up. We ended up losing 3 - 2 and I had to go to sixth form college the next day and face my class mates.

So I kept in relative remote contact with this monster love of my life. I was pretty much the odd one out at senior school, though I had unearthed two friends at school who were expressing their passion for the club; Keith Harris and Mark Williams. I would go on to attend a variety of matches with these first fellow supporters and start a trend of discovering Stoke City fans across the country throughout my life – always a treasure to find a kindred spirit.

I was 15, and was ready for my first ever game, I didn't know where or when it would be, I had little or no money, my dad worked 12 hour shifts at GEC every weekday and mum also worked cleaning at a local halls of residence just to make ends meet. My dad drew on his previous career as a chef to make sure we were never hungry. There were very few luxuries.

My older brother John, also working at GEC came to my rescue - but of course, this changed everything.

CHAPTER THREE
My first ever game

The 1975/76 season was taking fairly satisfactory shape. We ended up finishing twelfth with 15 wins, 7 away from home. By the time the FA Cup commenced on January 3rd, we were in the top half of the table. Among the several scalps we had taken were a famous double victory over Arsenal away 1-0, (Hudson) and at home 2 – 1 (Salmons, Greenhoff). Also a home victory over champions Leeds United 3 – 2. This match was the featured main event on Star Soccer. It was a stunning performance capped by a rocket of a volley by Jimmy Greenhoff to seal the win.

Other than Lincoln disposing of us in the League Cup, things were going pretty well. We were now 7th in the league with 29 points from 26 games (just 2 points for a win remember which in today's currency would equate to a 40 points haul). We had progressed to Round 4 of the FA Cup at the expense of Spurs in the 3rd round. After a 1 – 1 draw at White Hart Lane, we did the business in the replay which took place at home on the Saturday intended for Round 4 due to adverse weather conditions; the score was 2 – 1 with Moores and Salmons on target.

We already knew our opponents for the 4th Round, Manchester City at home, and excitement was building (in the Darling household particularly). My brother had agreed to take me to the evening fixture on 4th February 1976 together with his mate, Dick Webb.

I was experiencing a whole range of emotions. Apprehension, excitement and nervousness about the match and our tough

11

opponents and was maybe even a bit scared of this, my first live match opportunity. These feelings were to intensify during the evening.

As I said earlier, this major first step for me changed everything. I would be destined to visit parts of the UK I would never have otherwise contemplated visiting – and I include Stoke on Trent in this list.

I was a relatively long distance supporter, and it is relative as many fans embark on a much longer journey on match days than I do. The round trip from Rugby was 150 miles (50 miles less than my current round trip from my home in Northampton). This first game was an evening fixture at the Victoria Ground, my spiritual home for the next twenty plus years and from where some of my most vivid memories of match day experiences originate.

I hadn't really thought about the difference an evening game brings. Under floodlights with glistening turf I was just excited to be going. This would be my first ever trip to Stoke on Trent. I paid little attention to the surroundings, the rows of terraced housing and the economic challenges that the Potteries faced. My focus was purely on the game, whether we would get in and where we would stand. Over the years, through countless visits to the area, not just to the new and old grounds but also to meet friends and see local landmarks, I have come to appreciate the intrinsic working class heritage of the largest communities in the conurbation.

I had raced home from school and my brother, John, was also prompt after his shift at GEC (formerly English Electric). He had undergone an apprenticeship at "The Works" as a turbine fitter. (These turbines were used in Rolls Royce engines for power stations to generate electricity and in submarines around the world). I never really paid much attention to John's chosen trade at that point, although I now appreciate that he was a skilled engineer. He later joined the Metropolitan Police force and carved out a hard earned career before retiring early a few years ago with a recurring and still problematic knee injury.

Mum had dinner ready for us, and as it was a Wednesday, it was Mince and Tatties. This was devoured in an instant and we were ready to leave. I didn't see my dad before we left as he wasn't yet home from work. I knew he wasn't especially chuffed about us going - especially in John's three-wheeler car - but we were committed and I don't think I could have coped with the disappointment if we had called off at this stage.

So we set off at about 5.30pm in John's three wheeler Reliant, 21E, 1969, registration OVC 118H. It was a small hatchback version. My brother says it was a nice motor, in two tone green. It was basically Del Boy's car, except it wasn't yellow. John hadn't yet got a car driving license but the beauty of these models was that you could drive them on a motorcycle license – I never felt there was great logic in this as all of the instruments, foot pedals and gearstick were exactly like a conventional car. What on earth qualified someone to drive such a vehicle on the back of a motorcycle license god only knows! Some years later, I also passed my motorcycle test and while I was also therefore eligible to drive the Reliant, I politely declined.

We made our way up the M6 from our junction 1 to Junction 15. One of the reasons that John was interested in going to this game was because of his mate at work. John's mate Dick Webb was a Man City fan and was keen to go – a happy coincidence. I wasn't bothered, though I was grateful to Dick as it may well have been because of his suggestion that we were going to the game in the first place.

In the end Dick couldn't go, so it was just John and I. At the age of 15, just a few weeks before my 16th birthday and 5 years after my

13

interest in the club has been stimulated I was about to embark on my first ever Stoke City match. I guess because John is nine years older than me there wasn't much that we did together in those years, but for a very long time now, we have been much closer. John has attended a number of games with me across the years, despite the fact that Rugby rather than Football is his primary interest. John was a very good Rugby player. He played Tight Head Prop, No 3, and had trials that could have seen him play at a very high level. I would come to appreciate his scrummaging skills within a heaving crowd before the night was over.

The M6 seemed OK, much better than on dozens of other of occasions I can recall. This was before the M42 Junctions existed to complicate the traffic flow and we eased past Birmingham in good time. The M5 intersection is always a problem and while this slowed us down a little, it didn't delay us much. Soon we were past Junction 14 and then it seemed an age before we reached the exit at Junction 15, at 11 miles its one of the longest stretches between junctions on the motorway.

The moment we exited the motorway just before 7pm we hit the wall of traffic heading for the ground and snaking its way off the A500 and past Michelin slowly toward the very visible floodlights.

Before advanced LED technology, typical floodlights at football stadia were mounted on high stanchions with several large light bulbs strung together. They proved incredibly helpful on many occasions, giving us a steer of the general direction to the ground. It wasn't always reliable however. I remember going to Leicester for a night game some years later and as usual headed toward the floodlights with time slipping away, only to find that I was approaching the rugby rather than football ground (they weren't far apart though).

These days its all Sat Nav and Marshaled Parking, whereas

adjacent to the Victoria Ground was a maze of narrow streets with opportunities to park. As it happens parking was at a premium for this game and we were lucky to squeeze into a small space a little way from the ground and back toward Michelin – which meant a good getaway position. The benefit of having a very small vehicle meant we could get into a space that very few other cars would have attempted.

Time was ticking by as we left the car, and with throngs of others we made our way in the dark with about 15 minutes until kick off. It was a clear, cold evening. Very crisp air and perfect for football.

John seemed to know where he was going when we reached the ground. We found ourselves queuing to get into the Boothen End, not the entrance by the Boothen Paddock but the main turnstiles up the stairs at the back. I feared we had no chance of getting in, and was also not sure John knew which was the right entrance for Home fans. I was a novice, and so I thought I would try and be helpful and asked one of the guys in the melee/queue where the Stoke End was. He responded with a dismissive arm movement that suggested the other end. I told John but he reassured me we were going the right way.

Only around a year or so later I found out that the away fans stand on the Stoke End terrace. The guy I asked thought I was a Man City fan, not knowing where I was and asking for the "Stoke End" which I guess explains the welcome I received.

John and I were heading into a massive roofed terrace, The Boothen End. Our queue snaked right and up some stairs, left and then up more stairs and then the turnstiles came into view. We were 6 deep trying to edge into the funnel.

Our turn arrived as a very loud noise came from inside. Players were clearly on the pitch and the match was about to begin. We were in. I even managed to get a programme. (10p, I still have it). Inside the

15

Boothen End is cavernous and to reach the terrace we climbed another set of steps in the centre of the stand. We fought our way to the top and I expected to see football appearing before my eyes.

In reality there was none of it. We got to the top and couldn't move. It was like a living organism that ebbed and flowed, we were part of it, not in control, just responding and through it the occasional burst of electricity would result in ferocious activity - like when we get a corner! Yes, I came to learn that in the melee of the Boothen End, a corner would soon sort out any turf war disputes and correct things, though you had to react quickly.

John realised that while he could muscle a view of the pitch - or around 50% of it, I would be stuffed! Behind the main melee was another layer of terracing. The steps to this area were rammed and we would never reach them, however there was a large 3 ft step and someone allowed John to feed me under the barrier and into a fairly prime viewing position on the elevated step. From here I could observe both the match and the movements of the crowd. It was like a sea of people. There would be many occasions where my view was restricted and in truth I would see 60/75% of most matches but always the key moments as there are tactics to employ in these condensed crowd conditions that I quickly learned.

It was the same either getting a drink or going to the toilet – far different from nowadays where there are polite single queues. Other than at the odd away game where you need all your guile to get to the bar or sometimes the gents. The conditions are similar to those still found at Goodison Park, Everton's home ground and they aren't much better at Anfield.

The space at the front of this higher layer of terracing by the bar was occupied mainly by younger supporters of my age and perhaps a bit younger, where they could see and be kind of looked after from a safe distance. It was still scary. I was pushed, pressed, jostled throughout and the score was 0 - 0.

Years later I attended a *Dammed* gig at the Humming Bird in Birmingham and being in the Boothen End felt similar to that. I got a real buzz from this and was well equipped to cope with the carnage.

It struck me that there was of course, no commentary, no action replay of key moments how on earth did people know who had the ball! Its all completely obvious of course, but this was my first experience. I soon acclimatized to it and the coordinated chants which I had also never experienced before. And yes, even today the referee is still a "wanker"! In fact probably even more so today as referees have acquired celebrity status and do appear to like to show the live and TV audiences that they are on the pitch. I'm talking about you Mike Dean.

My memories of the game range from clear as day moments that I will never forget to a murky picture of events. There was a huge crowd of 38,073 which remains the largest home attendance at Stoke I have ever witnessed. I was so immersed in the occasion, with the crowd noise and movements, I was almost hypnotised or mesmerised.

In the first half Mike Pejic was sent off for head-butting Willie Donachie. it wasn't too long before parity was restored as Donachie himself was dismissed for an ongoing series of offences; so 10 versus 10.

It was my dream to see Peter Shilton between the posts and witness first hand the electrifying partnership between Alan Hudson and Jimmy Greenhoff. Indeed all the Stoke City players that night have a special place in my heart.

Half Time arrived at 0 – 0 and there was no way I was moving, even if I had wanted to; I was locked into my position and craving a

17

home victory.

On the Manchester City team sheet were some big names. Dave Watson and Mike Doyle marshaled the centre of defence both of whom would arrive to have successful spells at Stoke in later years. Up front Joe Royle, Asa Hartford and Peter Barnes were leading the line.

As the second half wore on it remained a tight game with few chances. The expectation in the crowd was intensifying and excitement levels were visibly building. There was a growing sense that this was the time to really press for a winner. An away replay at Maine Road in the event of a draw would be exceptionally tough.

For much of the game I was adrenalin fuelled by the atmosphere, but also conscious that I could be crushed at any moment if things got out of hand. I entertained fears of us scoring, there being a push and me being squashed against the barrier against which I was already firmly pressed. Whilst I briefly dreaded that possibility, as time went on I dreamed of that winner, just one move that would result in a winning goal, even though it would be at the opposite end of the ground, the Stoke End. (Goals scored at the Boothen End being the ultimate of course).

We moved toward the last 5 minutes or so and we had a great move down the left and in an instant after a low cross it was in! The Boothen End went mental, I didn't die against the barrier, but, unfortunately the goal was ruled out for offside. I felt robbed, angry, cheated, my stomach was tight, cramped.

The noise levels ramped up. Wow! I had never experienced anything like this before. We kept the pressure on, retained the noise levels and suddenly I wasn't in the slightest bit concerned about my certain death in the event that we did actually score the winner. I also did something I have only ever done two or three times ever - I looked to the heavens, or in this case the iron roof frame of the Boothen End stand and begged for divine intervention. This wasn't normal behaviour on my part, just pure desperation - I would have done anything for a winning goal at that moment.

With time running out Terry Conroy continued to race down the right and sent a great low cross into the box, I didn't know who picked it up at the time, but I later learned it was Jimmy Greenhoff. It seemed to take an age, but Jimmy slammed it in and wild celebrations began.

I was so caught up with the mental celebrations taking place, it took me a while to realise my brother was calling me to climb under the bar and make an exit with just a minute or so to go. I complied, though would have loved to have been there at the final whistle and the end of a magical experience.

The journey home was quite quiet, I don't remember much conversation, there was no need. It was a perfect occasion. I was privileged. We arrived home just as TV highlights of the match were coming to a close on the Big Match and celebrations were taking place. I watched the last few minutes and went to bed content, absolutely knackered but still buzzing.

All this was thanks to John, and I have repaid the favour with various football trips. I hoped that taking him to Wembley for our first ever FA Cup final against the same team, Man City, might have completed the remarkable 35 year journey with the same result. Despite another request for divine intervention, sadly this was not to be.

CHAPTER FOUR
We support our local team (not)

Let's be clear, I have never supported my local team, other than attending the odd game to watch VS Rugby when they got to rounds 1 & 2 of the FA Cup and over the last couple of decades, being interested in how the Cobblers, Northampton Town (where I live) are getting on.

So it feels a bit strange to me when our chant is *"we support our local team"*, usually its when playing Manchester United or the like who have a broader fan base which at times feels like its only a minority of fans who are from the town or city where the club is based. This is definitely the case at Old Trafford where my experience is that its full of tourists on match days – which is great for revenue, but doesn't help create the kind of atmosphere that delivers genuine home advantage.

The best example of this is from our own stadium where we made the Britannia Stadium (the Brit) a real Bear Pit and a place that opposing teams never looked like they enjoyed (even if they occasionally won). Its impossible to quantify the number of points that this helped us win, especially in seasons where there was clear and present danger of losing our Premier League status. It wasn't just the opening reception and general noise levels that were so impressive. It was the way that the crowd seemed to sense, sometimes well into the second half of games that the players needed the boost and responded with the kind of support and backing that most clubs dream of. In that regard, Tony Pulis really benefitted as our manager and leveraged off this incredible advantage.

Stoke City is a long way off being and has never been my local team. My current round trip from Northampton is 200 miles to home games (though I benefit from many away games especially in London where it's a very straightforward journey). The closest trip I ever had from home was around 85 miles when I was living in Birmingham and was surrounded by Blues, Villa and Baggies fans. There are a great many who travel much further both within the UK and from abroad, to support our team, and I wonder what their thoughts are when they hear the chant?

When growing up in Rugby, the most prominent local team of any note was Coventry City, 12 miles away. I really hated them, partly jealousy and partly other reasons which follow. I still hate them today – though I am glad to say there is no jealousy involved. They currently find themselves in a perilous position. Oh dear.

To many, they seem an innocuous club that haven't really troubled Stoke City or many other clubs for that matter. It causes some surprise and intrigue when I announce my feelings about them – something I continue to do regularly. Here's my story, make your own mind up but I promise you, nothing will change mine.

During the calamitous 1976/77 season, my first as a supporter attending matches after my emotional introduction at the 4th Round FA Cup match against Man City earlier in the year, we were relegated along with Spurs (who finished bottom of the league) and Sunderland. Spurs finished on 33 points, we had 34 equal with Sunderland who had a far superior goal difference.

This particular season was calamitous for a number of reasons which I have painfully described in Chapter Five. For the purpose of this chapter, Coventry City were also struggling. It became a dog fight between a few clubs at the bottom, and while our fate had been sealed, Coventry City, Bristol City and Sunderland were fighting it out on the last game of the season to avoid the third and final relegation place. It went down to the wire and ended up with Coventry playing at home to Bristol City and Sunderland travelling to Everton.

I can't remember why these last and crucial games were being played midweek after the rest of the season was over. I was listening with great interest on the radio, where annoyingly I could easily get a good signal for this local game opposed to the trouble I had getting a Radio Stoke signal.

Sunderland ended up losing 3 - 0 at Everton but would still stay up unless it was a draw at Coventry, as they had a better goal difference of -8 opposed to Coventry's -11 and Bristol City's -10.

The Coventry game had mysteriously kicked of 15 minutes late, when Jimmy Hill, Coventry City Chairman ordered the delay due to "crowd congestion" (oh yeah!). With a good 10 minutes still to play and the teams level at 2 – 2, it was announced over the tannoy that Sunderland had lost to Everton and with a draw enough for both clubs to avoid relegation, play virtually stopped and the game drifted to its obvious conclusion. Sunderland were relegated, joining Stoke and Spurs.

But that's only a small part of it. Jimmy Hill's actions during that game to manipulate the outcome really got under my skin. He fulfilled many roles in the game; player, trade union leader, coach, manager, chairman, television executive, presenter (regularly hosting Match of the Day), analyst and assistant referee. He campaigned for an end to the Football League's maximum wage in 1961.

More irritatingly he changed the home kit's colours to sky blue and penned the club song "The Sky Blue Song" sung to the tune of the Eton Boating Song – horrible.

He innovated the match day programme, introduced pre match entertainment to encourage fans to arrive early (perhaps he should have focused on developing the entertainment on view after the first whistle had been blown) and commissioned the first English all-seater-stadium. To me with my deep seated love of the Boothen End and standing on terraces at away matches, this was too much to bear and eventually this led to the revolution of stadia in England.

Jimmy was a visionary, who did many great things for the game. He probably didn't deserve the dogs abuse given to him when Stoke visited after promotion in 1979, we had beaten them 3 – 2 at home on the first day of that season and visited Highfield Road on November 3rd winning well 3 – 1 through an own goal and others by Adrian Heath and Garth Crooks. Life was looking up.

Coventry's Highfield Road stadium had become a bit of a dump. The main home support gathered in the lower tier of terracing called the West End, which used to be shared with away fans. The other end was a strange construction with an open ended terrace called the spion and cop.

Earlier, during the 1976/77 season of calamity, we lost 5 - 2 at Coventry. They were 3 - 0 up within 10 mins, and Peter Shilton (one of the best goalkeepers on the planet) had a shocker. There were two other things I remember from the game. Firstly, the guys I had dragged along with me (Simon Poole, Adrian Barlow, Colin Flannagan and Graham Gibson) ended up catching the wrong train home, and instead of the 10 minute journey to Rugby, found ourselves in Watford an hour later. Great! Second, and this one is weird, I am certain that Coventry played in an all red strip with a funny stripe on it and we played in sky blue colours - maybe it was a dream, you know the really bad kind.

As my team was cast into oblivion (or so I thought), Coventry continued their escapology, I won't dwell but here are a few highlights. In the 1982/83 season they finished one place and a single point above the relegation zone. It wasn't so bad, at least one sky blue coloured team went down; Manchester City.

In 1983/84 they were close again finishing one place and two points off relegation.

The second worst season for me was to follow in 1984/85. In this season, they needed to win all of their last three games to have a chance of staying up. In between their game against Luton (which they won 1 – 0) they were playing Stoke at the Victoria Ground then finally the new League Champions Everton at Highfield Road.

Finally, we would have the honor of sending this shower down, it was meant to be. Actually it would mean bringing them down with us as we endured the worst top flight season in our history. With just 17 points from 42 games we were bottom of the league by a mile. A massive 34 points off safety and a negative goal difference of 67.

Surely you are thinking this must be the season of true calamity, and of course that would be right, its just the circumstances of the 1976/77 season that made that so painful for me. But, we could take Coventry City with us, a draw at home would be enough.

I wasn't at the game on 17th May 1985, in fact not many were, the crowd was 6,930 and that included a healthy away following from Houdini City. Stuart Pearce scored a 66th minute penalty to give the visitors a chance of staying up and then with six minutes to go we were awarded a penalty of our own, facing the Boothen End and Ian Painter, our top goal scorer (with just six goals), stepped up to make it 1 – 1. Unfortunately for the world of football, his penalty struck

24

the underside of the bar and rebounded to safety - we had let then off the hook.

I didn't know at the time that apparently the ball had clearly crossed the line after hitting the underside of the bar and I resigned myself to life in the lower reaches of the football leagues. I wasn't giving up hope on Coventry joining us however as they had to play First Division Champions Everton in their last game and had to win. No prizes for guessing the outcome as they won 4 – 1, finishing a single point above the relegation zone (again) and by now I had relinquished all hope of their relegation and demise.

I am not sure who remarked that if they had painted the Titanic sky blue, it would never have gone down!

Things got a lot worse for me before they got better. We drew Coventry at home in the 1987 FA Cup 5th round, a 31,255 crowd roaring the Potters on and we gave them a good game. With less than ten minutes remaining, Micky Gynn was sent through and despite being offside, scored to make it 1 - 0, the eventual score line.

After beating Sheffield Wednesday in the quarter final, Coventry got the easiest draw available in the semis facing Leeds at Hillsborough. They won a tight affair 3 - 2 and were in the final where Tottenham awaited them. The only good news was that Tottenham were rampant and with Clive Allen firing on all cylinders, at least they would embarrass Coventry in the final to bring about some justice.

Allen scored after just two minutes of the final and I was satisfied it would become a rout. I wanted a cricket score. What followed however was quite painful, so I will skip some of the details. Coventry ran out 3 - 2 winners with an own goal from Gary Mabbutt sealing the victory.

25

There is however always a silver lining. Due to the dreadful antics of rioting Liverpool fans at Heysel stadium in Brussels a year earlier, which caused the death of 39 fans, English football clubs were banned from playing in European competitions for five years (Liverpool were awarded a six year ban). At least I didn't have to endure Coventry City in Europe.

The following season brought about some further comfort and joy. The cup holders drew lowly Non League Sutton United, in the 3rd round and were beaten in embarrassing style. Cup winners dumped out by non league opposition. Now that's more like it, maybe this was the start of the big slide! We of course also exited in the 3rd Round at the hands of Liverpool.

So that's mainly why I hate them - oh and also because of events such as, when playing Crystal Palace in 1980, Clive Allen scored a spectacular free kick against them. The ball had struck the angle of the stanchion inside the goal and rebounded out at pace. Decision? No goal. Give me strength.

Sometimes in life you have to play the long game (no that's not a reference to Tony Pulis tactics), you have to be patient and wait for things that go around, to come around. I waited patiently.

The tide turned on 5th May 2001 the last game of the season, we were playing Swindon at home and a win would seal our play off place in the Third Division. Coventry were playing away at Aston Villa where only a win would save them. I expected them to get the win and within 25 minutes they were 2 – 0 up. We won comfortably in the end 4 – 1 and were safely in the play-offs. My interest was elsewhere and the news of Villa's comeback and a third goal to give them a 3 – 2 lead meant I could hold it in no longer. I don't know what my neighbours in the Boothen End thought about my uncontrollable celebrations that were nothing to do with my team reaching the play-offs. I was experiencing pure relief, my mates knew, and in my heart I knew it was going to get tougher for them in Division 2. It did.

We eventually scraped our way back into Division 2, now called the Championship and made hard work of staying in it. Our away game at Coventry near the end of the 2002/03 season was one we needed to win. I was in a hospitality area with some mates and other guests and there was a quiz beforehand in the lounge. One of the questions was who scored the winner in the FA Cup 5th round at Stoke in 1987. Of course it was Micky Gynn as I mentioned earlier, so when they announced the answers, I stood up and shouted "he was off-side!" which didn't go down too well, but was just too good an opportunity to resist. Funny really, I went to another game there also in hospitality (where we lost 3 - 1) and they had the same quiz questions, and I performed my "off-side" piece again. It was fun and I think the MC was the same person as on the first occasion and looked even more pissed off second time around.

Anyway back to the game, we weren't great, but won a soft penalty which big Chris Iwelumo stepped up to take. He hit the post, the ball rebounded hit their keeper, Montgomery, on the arse and went in. We won 1 - 0 and did stay up that year.

Coventry had now moved into the Ricoh Arena, an impressive stadium nearer Nuneaton than Coventry. It was a bit like the Britannia, in the middle of nowhere. In the 2007/08 season, we were promoted to the Premier League, something I thought I would never see and we won at Coventry with goals from Liam Lawrence and Ricardo Fuller.

In our final game against Leicester at home, we needed a single point to secure promotion. In fact in the end if we had lost, we would still have gone up. We drew 0 - 0 and celebrations ensued. For a change I wasn't thinking about Coventry City, though I soon was as I realised that if Leicester had taken all 3 points against us that day, we would still have been promoted to the Premier League (after our 23 year absence), Leicester would have stayed up, and Coventry City, now dancing on the trap door of the Championship (old Division 2) would have been relegated. They had finished their characteristic one point and a single place above the relegation places.

I wasn't to be disappointed for long, they were relegated again on 21st April 2012 after suffering a final day home defeat to already relegated Doncaster Rovers. They lost their Ricoh Arena ground in 2013 and as a result were forced to play home games at Northampton Town's stadium, in my home town. This was most embarrassing for Coventry City and I was enjoying this almost as much as my own teams progress in the Premier League.

What goes around did come back around, the waiting game was well worth it and in terms of supporting my local team, I was rooting for the Cobblers (Northampton Town) when they met in the FA Cup in 2016 and won at the Ricoh.

As for Coventry, they did return to play games at the impressive Ricoh Arena and as I first compose this chapter they were 24th and bottom in League One (that's the old Division 3) and facing either relegation or another edgy battle to avoid League Two (old Division 4).

On 14th April 2017, Coventry City were relegated to the fourth and lowest tier of the English Football League.

Strangely I didn't get as much satisfaction from that and in speaking to a friend who is a Coventry fan, he asked how I would feel if, as he expects to happen, Coventry City are liquidated and disappear entirely. I wanted to say, yes, great the end of a journey into oblivion that I hoped they would complete, however, that's not how I really felt. I wanted suffering, oh yes, but what I really wanted most was to know that my club had become infinitely superior. That's how we stand today.

So for Coventry City fans reading this book (and I know there will be a few who have already pre-ordered a copy from me) I don't want you to go bust and disappear. I want to draw you in the League and FA Cup and give you a right old thrashing.

Coventry did have a rare moment to savour during their latest season of calamity. This was in the final of the CheckaTrade competition where 40,000 Sky Blue fans packed Wembley where they defeated Oxford United 2 – 1 and lifted the trophy.

On the day of the game, I messaged my Coventry City fan friend Eugene and even meant it when I wished him a great day out. He responded after the match as follows:

"Thanks Brian. The sun shone, a perfect Sky Blue day! Now to focus on Div 4 footie, no ground, no academy, no players and no training ground (being sold for house development)!"

Oh well.

CHAPTER FIVE
1976/77 Season of Calamity

Let's be honest, this could quite easily be my longest chapter. There have been many seasons that could be described as calamitous.

The relegation season of 1984/5 where we were stranded bottom of the First Division is an obvious candidate. We had finished the previous season in style beating Wolves 4 – 0 on the final day to guarantee survival, all four scored by Paul Maguire. Maguire started his career with Shrewsbury Town and helped them win the Third Division title in 1976. He was sold to Stoke for a sizeable transfer fee of £262,000 in 1980, aged 24. His appearance and four goal performance against Wolves was his last appearance for the club as he moved first to Tacoma Stars in the United States and later Port Vale in 1985.

Stoke had appointed Bill Asprey as Manager. He had been the caretaker manager and architect of our great escape during the previous 1983/84 season. Unfortunately the heroics, which included a return to the club for the inspirational Alan Hudson, couldn't be repeated and it was clear from an early stage that goals were going to be a big problem. We scored just five goals in our first six games, conceded ten and had won just once. In November, we lost all four games scoring just once. It got worse, and we didn't score again after Boxing Day (when we famously beat Man Utd 2 – 1 at home) until 23rd March. The Boxing Day win was our third and final win of the season and we lost all of our last ten games (including that game against Coventry City I have described in Chapter Four).

Surely this was it 1984/85, the Season of Calamity?

No.

Neither were the 1989/90 or 1990/91 seasons, even though they were respectively, the season which saw us relegated to the third Division followed by the season when we finished 14th in the third Division, our lowest ever finishing position.

For me, the season which ranks as the season of absolute calamity was 1976/77. I had built a very strong emotional relationship with the club by this time and attended my first game in the cup against Manchester City in February. I was ready to become a fully fledged supporter attending games on my own (and with a variety of mates).

It felt as though the entire foundations of my relationship with the club which had only so recently been cemented were being dismantled before my eyes; and yet to me a young and relatively long distance supporter, I didn't realise what was going on until the roof genuinely did cave in.

My first game of this season was Aston Villa at home. Things were going reasonably well with a respectable seven points from our opening seven games. We were mid table. We managed to defeat these local Midlands rivals 1 – 0 in front of a healthy crowd of 29,652. Villa had some top players in their ranks including Dennis Mortimer, Brian Little and Andy Gray. Terry Conroy scored the winner and Peter Shilton saved a penalty from the usually very reliable Ray Graydon. During this game I also recall Alan Dodd, our defender, carrying an escaped dog off the pitch!

We followed this up at my next game three weeks later with a similar 1 – 0 win at home to Derby when new striker John Tudor nabbed the winner in front of the Boothen End (the first goal I ever saw Stoke score at my end of the ground). I was beginning to believe

31

that we would win every game 1 – 0, it had now happened 3 times. My enduring memory of this game was interplay between Alan Hudson and Jimmy Greenhoff (who was now my ultimate hero). I cherished the opportunity to watch Hudson and Greenhoff play together and despite the turmoil taking place behind the scenes, I was mesmerised by the partnership and the understanding they possessed. As for Derby, they still had some wonderful players such as Colin Todd, Archie Gemmill, Bruce Rioch and Charlie George making our victory a really good one.

We carried on gaining points in low scoring matches, with home form proving vital. However things were starting to fall apart at the club in dramatic fashion and for me my world was being torn apart. I never imagined that this would be the last time I would ever see my heroes Greenhoff and Hudson play together.

The storm damage caused to the roof of the Butler Street Stand the previous Winter meant a huge repair bill only partly covered by insurance. The club needed to find £250,000 toward the repair and rebuilding costs.

Five key players were sold to raise funds. Sean Haslegrave (£35,000 to Nottingham Forest), Ian Moores (£75,000 to Tottenham), Mike Pejic (£140,000 to Everton) and the real body blows to the club, its supporters and to me very personally, Alan Hudson (£200,000 to Arsenal) and the worst of all, my favourite player Jimmy Greenhoff (£100,000 to Man Utd).

Jimmy had played 338 times for the club scoring almost 100 goals and he was idolised by supporters. I was totally gutted. The fee of £100,000 was also a disgrace for a player of his obvious ability and while it wouldn't have made me feel much better at least his true value should have been realised.

I felt thoroughly let down and never thought to challenge or reconcile the explanations given and recorded by the club – I was in shock.

The Encyclopaedia of Stoke City 1868 – 1994 suggests that the repair cost was £250,000 of which approximately one third was recovered from the insurers. That means around £170,000 was the funding gap. Proceeds from the player sales totaled £550,000. I felt betrayed.

All six of our wins pre Christmas had been at home, and when that form also began to desert us, the fast signs of decline were all too clear to see.

By the time we played West Brom at the Victoria Ground on 18th December (my next live game), we had 16 points from 16 games but the gap between us and the bottom three narrowed rapidly. Only Mike Pejic of the five players to leave was still at the club. We lost 2 – 0, the first goals I had ever seen us concede. One brighter moment was that I saw Garth Crooks for the first time who was to become a new favourite with the fans, but without possessing the class of Jimmy Greenhoff.

We didn't win again until 16th February (against Coventry at home) and were struggling badly now, gradually slipping down the league. It was still tight in the lower reaches of Division One and still quite possible for us to dig ourselves out of trouble.

I attended three of the last four away games of the season; including Birmingham City where we lost 2 – 0 (I had left the ground a minute or two early at 1 – 0 and we were never in the game). At Coventry City we lost 5 – 2 and I also missed the final goal in this game. Then two weeks later at West Brom, where we actually took the lead and it was looking good. Unfortunately we went on to lose 3 – 1, and again, for the third match in succession I had left a little early and missed the last goal to seal the 3 – 1 defeat.

We needed a result at Aston Villa in our final game of the season, but couldn't achieve it. We were relegated.

It wasn't the end of the turmoil. Tony Waddington, who had spent 25 years at the club, 15 of those as manager, was dismissed.

While Peter Shilton's departure wasn't until the start of the 1977 season, the dye had been cast by the previous campaign and it was no real surprise when he left to join Nottingham Forest for £240,000. He went on to achieve major League and European success with them as well as recording the highest number of appearances for England, 125 caps.

I have always remained an advocate of Peter Shilton. His England appearance record is amazing in itself and it would have been dozens more caps had the England management team (Don Revie in particular) recognised that he was head and shoulders above Ray Clemence who was being alternated with Shilton in the England goal. Ultimately, Clemence's mistakes became too much and Shilton became the undisputed number 1.

Revie didn't seem to understand that while Clemence was keeping clean sheets for Liverpool (having to make very few saves in the process), Shilton was playing out of his skin while Stoke were losing 2 or 3 nil.

I hope the appearance record is never broken, however Wayne Rooney is now approaching this milestone. My views on Rooney are well known among my fellow group of Stoke supporters. Rooney has played 119 times at the time of writing, yet has been subbed off 57 times and has managed 8934 minutes in an England shirt.

34

Peter was on the pitch far longer, playing 10725 minutes. It's a bit in the balance at the moment, Rooney's form suggests he shouldn't get near the side and his record in competitions with England is dreadful. He quite possibly cost us the World Cup in Germany 2006 (kicking out petulantly at Ronaldo in the quarter final match against Portugal and getting himself sent off). I was there to witness his disgrace. On the flip side, he is still captain of England which suggests that Southgate may well select him for a number of further "part time" appearances. Lets hope not!

So, back to the season of calamity. The combination of the timing of all this turmoil (so soon after I had been initiated as a life long fan) and the depth of the consequences, with key player and managerial departures, plus the resultant relegation means that, for me, this was the worst ever year since I started supporting the club.

I remember friends (some fellow Stoke fans) saying that maybe relegation and a year or two in the Second Division might be the best thing for the club. This didn't seem too ridiculous at the time, though being cast into the wilderness with no visible prospect of returning is most definitely the worst thing possible. In today's Premier League where nearly 80% of the Club's gross income comes from Broadcasting Income (around £80m currently and rising!) the prospect of relegation is almost unbearable.

CHAPTER SIX
The Banking Industry

Look, I am a Banker, always have been. I know its not everyone's favourite profession and its always good to bash a Banker every now and again, (some really deserve it, believe me). After we replaced the lowest of the low in terms of most hated profession (Estate Agents) in the recent financial and Banking crisis, the perception hasn't really improved, even though it is only a small minority who have caused the issues that gave rise to these feelings.

I remember in 2010, about two years into the Financial Crisis and recession, how some of my colleagues at Lloyds were telling stories of lying about their profession when asked by people down the pub or at school parent evenings. Stories of how their children were subject to bullying because their mum or dad was working in a Bank. I personally never experienced that, I think I would have been quite defensive. As the recession deepened and the behaviour of the Banks (including Lloyds where I worked from 2008) deteriorated, my feelings of pride in the workplace had become bruised and battered.

My colleagues and I had become accustomed to showing real pride in the Banks we were working for. We would stick up for them when challenged about their mortgage rate or personal loan terms. We could handle that and were always inclined to defend our employers. So the shift was tough to take and the acronym PRIDE, most brilliantly captured by Nationwide's colleague agenda, was no longer in frequent use.

You might think it difficult to relate a 37 year Banking career with a far more understandable passion for Stoke City. I really did weave this into my personal operating model and as I became more senior, built my working calendar around my football and more specifically my Stoke City obsession. This was far more than just admitting to colleagues along the way that I was a Stoke fan who bunked off early a few times to get to the match. I would almost never deliver internal presentations to colleagues without multiple mentions of my team. I would use every analogy possible to open the door to the subject and once through that door, I was there to use my contagious state to infect everyone I could.

I used to sow seeds everywhere and then harvest all opportunities that grew: and grow they did. Finding myself in leadership positions where, at various times, I managed teams of colleagues and customers across the UK led to a wide range of acquaintances. This gave me all the rope I needed to synchronize work engagements with Stoke City fixtures.

It's genuinely a part of the story. It was at least partly responsible for making my unremarkable Banking career, memorable. Regardless of where I was working and what my domestic circumstances were, this large portion of my life was always punctuated by Stoke City performances across the decades.

I also want to tell it straight about the Banking industry. I want you to feel the solidarity and the intense pride that I enjoyed at certain points of my career so that you know how good being a Banker can be. The flip side of course is the sheer purgatory and disconsolation that is part and parcel of working in a Bank through periods of recession. I will give you my take on the financial crisis of 2007/08 and how badly the Banks responded in this period. My firm belief is that it could have been far more positive and lucrative for the Banks if they had operated differently. So, from positions of relative seniority, I will share my personal thoughts and give an insight to what was really going on inside the Banking industry during this crucial period.

I recently left Banking after 37 years in the profession. I figured that that was plenty long enough in an industry that had undergone massive and turbulent change and had found itself in a place where there was little room for intuition, instinct, creativity and fun. In short it had lost its soul, and I promise you it did have one, once upon a time.

My passion was building the business, working with customers, building relationships and it was at Nationwide where I had most opportunity to personally direct the style and nature of how this would be conducted. I encouraged and empowered my team to deliver brilliant basics (the essential things that must be correctly done within any Bank to deliver the key parts of whatever the product was that customers needed) with magic touches (this is where we had the ability to shine brighter than any competitor). It was the gold dust that made the customer experience memorable, for all the right reasons. This could mean delivering early, exceeding customer expectations, taking time to celebrate the completion of the deal, before moving relentlessly on to the next one. Things that didn't always cost much but made the customer feel special, demonstrating that Bankers could be good, sensitive people. In the process, this ethos made my team feel special and at times we were also very successful.

Shocks in the Banking industry have always led to an over reaction and an adjustment of behaviour and policy of a disproportionate level. The latest Banking crisis known as the 2008 Financial Crisis was no exception in fact it prompted even deeper, and I would suggest even more disproportionate responses by major UK and International Banks.

So where did this all begin and manifest itself on the UK? I will keep this brief history short and cut to the chase. Its beginnings were in the subprime mortgage market in the USA. Subprime is a fancy word for higher risk mortgage lending, and by this I mean *really* high risk mortgage lending. Bankers being Bankers found a way to bundle up in portfolios of thousands of these subprime loans and sold them off to investors, offering high returns. The risk was disguised in the portfolio combining thousands of smaller loans and by adding "liquidity" lines (relatively small cash reserves in case of difficulty with some of the loans). Investors convinced themselves it was a reasonable risk for a good return. The market was incredibly buoyant and remained on a positive trajectory. It seemed as though nothing could fail and that, it was all going to be fine; when in hindsight it pretty much never was.

So when the inflated house price bubble burst in the US, property values of these predominantly residential properties plummeted. But how did this activity taking place on a huge scale in the US affect the UK financial markets? Many reasons, here are a few. Investors in these subprime packages included big UK institutions and many Banks internationally. They were all about to lose a packet. Excessive risk taking by Banks such as Lehman Brothers caused their collapse on 15th September 2008, sending shockwaves across global financial markets. The fear was that others such as Merrill Lynch, Freddie Mac, Fannie Mae, HBoS, Royal Bank of Scotland, Bradford & Bingley, Fortis, Alliance & Leicester and others would follow.

There were still plenty of other solvent Banks to turn to but the problem was one of lack of confidence. The fear of the unknown. What else was being hidden or similarly disguised by the Banks? This breakdown in trust and confidence caused the *Interbank* market to seize up.

The Interbank market is lending and borrowing that takes place between financial institutions and was a major source of their liquidity, or put another way their ability to trade as Banks. Traditionally Banks had lent money for mortgages and a variety of commercial enterprises over medium and long-term periods, typically upwards of ten years and in some instances far longer. They funded this partly through customer deposits but mainly through Interbank loans which they rolled over on a regular basis. These loans were predominantly of a much shorter term than the bulk of the customer lending Banks had committed to.

So they lent long term (to home buyers like you and I and to business enterprises) and funded this by borrowing the money themselves over a shorter term. It had become common place to do this and for many years, while short term Interbank lending was available at very fine margins, it was a very profitable method of funding the long term lending.

That is until the Interbank market effectively seized up. It never entirely closed but rapidly adjusted the terms upon which it would lend. Costs soared and the fine margins that existed became far more expensive and Banks had few alternatives other than to keep borrowing on the higher rates.

Some Banks, who were believed to have been heavily participating in investing in sub prime found it hard to access funding in the market, or at best managed it only at exorbitant interest rates. It was like what happens in pass the parcel when the music stops; and Banks had become reliant on the music never stopping.

So all of a sudden, Banks became really interested in building up their levels of retail deposits and for the first time in a while needed to pay competitive levels to attract our cash. All of the attempts to seduce us with fixed rate savings products and bonds, were aimed at securing the liquidity and funding they needed, and so that they had less reliance on the now expensive Interbank markets.

In the UK the first key collapse was at Northern Rock. The Bank of England stepped in to deliver emergency funding which immediately saw their share price plummet from over £6 to £2. A global and deep UK recession was looming. This affected house prices and commercial Real Estate significantly. Sterling followed suit falling from nearly 2.1US$ to the £1 to less than 1.5US$ to each £1.

That's the potted background, but only scratches the surface. Massive turmoil was to follow.

By the way, while all this was going on, Stoke found the wherewithal to gain automatic promotion to the promised land of the Premier League, in complete contrast to the events in the financial markets of the world. On the day Lehmans collapsed we drew 1 – 1 at Hull City. Then, while Northern Rock was running out of cash to dispense to customers queuing around the block at most of its branches, we beat Plymouth Argyle 3 – 2 at home with Ricardo Fuller and Liam Lawrence on target (and some help from an own goal).

CHAPTER SEVEN
Becoming a Banker 1979/1990

My banking career was performed in three segments, beginning with 11 years at Barclays. This was followed by 18 years at Nationwide, which was largely successful and enjoyable. My final banking segment was 8 years at Lloyds as the take over of HBoS took place.

Barclays

I left College in Summer 1979, a great year for Stoke which saw us promoted back to the First Division (now Premier League) after finishing third in Division Two. This was made possible on an emotional final day of the season away at Notts County where, among over 15,000 Stoke fans who had descended on Nottingham, I witnessed an injury time winner. Paul Richardson's diving header sent us up, instead of Sunderland who were also winning and would have been promoted instead of us, but for our very late goal.

I had achieved an Ordinary National Diploma in Business Studies (which I saw as an easier ride than A Levels that it broadly corresponds to). I always felt it was quite a rubbish title for the result of a two-year full time A Level standard course, "Ordinary", surely they could have attached a more inspiring label. Anyway, having just about scraped through in a couple of core subjects on the course, I never contemplated University and started applying for jobs.

Living in Rugby and having no job meant getting to Stoke games wasn't easy. I had a 100cc Honda, but that wasn't really up to 150 mile round trips to home games, so I tried to convince friends (with a car) it would be a great day out to drive to Stoke for a match. I had limited success though my friend Bruce did relent and took Steve, another good mate and myself, up to Stoke for the visit of Everton on 8th September 1979. We lost 3 – 2 in a good game where we came back from 2 – 0 down to level before half time and succumbed in the second half. This was our first season after promotion. The game I was looking forward to was away at Coventry, whom we had beaten 3 – 2 on the opening day of the season at home, giving us a flying start.

I applied to a few local Banks, you know the usual names in those days, Barclays, Midland (now HSBC), Nat West (now RBS with Nat West as a sub brand) and Lloyds. My dad was very keen that I also apply for a role at Coutts & Co who had a glitzy office on the Strand in London and while I felt this was a complete and utter waste of time, I sent my letter off to them as well.

Within a couple of weeks I had been invited to two interviews, one at the local branch of Barclays in Rugby, on North Street and the second at Coutts & Co on the Strand. My dad was chuffed, vindicated. I was a bit puzzled. The Coutts interview was the first one I attended, and I had bought a new suit (mid brown, pin striped, three piece from Burtons) a brown stripy shirt and used one of my dad's ties, also new brown shoes. It was actually ok, quite smart and while nervous and without any real thought or preparation I headed for London to my interview.

As I came out of Charing Cross station the Coutts building was unmistakable, an imposing fully glass fronted ten or so storey building that doubled as their flagship branch and their Head Office. I was greeted by someone dressed as a butler, black suit, bowler hat etc who ushered me into the building and towards reception. They had some impressive escalators, which took me up to the office level where I was introduced to my three, yes three, interviewers. My memory about the content is a bit vague, however I do remember

43

that they advised me, toward the end of the meeting that, if I were to be selected, there were some regulations about required dress for employees at Coutts. The first was that a black suit was required (oh dear), the second was that black shoes were required (bugger) and that only white shirts and black ties were permitted (taxi for Mr Darling). Subconsciously I looked myself up and down and knew it was well and truly over, you know, like the third goal against us playing Manchester United away in our first season in the Premier League in a game that we were never going to recover from the first one, let alone two and then there's a third.

I felt like a right tit, and while my average interview content could perhaps be excused, the complete lack of awareness of appropriate dress code was unforgivable. I was relieved to leave the building and hoped that, at some point long into the distant future, I might be able to look back and appreciate the experience. Not likely.

My only other interview (with Barclays Bank) was next, just a few days after the Coutts debacle. I attended in the same outfit as it was the only suit I possessed. The interview went ok. It was altogether more relaxed and chatty and in the process I told the single interviewer about the Coutts interview. At what felt like the end of the interview and to my surprise and amazement, the manager, Peter Warrilow, a straightforward enough kind of guy, offered me a job there and then.

It threw me a bit, although I remember thinking this job hunt business isn't all that hard. I don't know what possessed me to do so, but I told him that I was still waiting to hear from Coutts and so could I let him know after that! Luckily for me, he agreed. In a few days the letter from Coutts arrived and politely advised me that there was not a position they could offer me. This came as absolutely no surprise. I contacted Mr Warrilow and accepted his offer at Barclays, where I started as a junior in the machine room in September 1979.

I will never entirely know, but I firmly believe that my reference to the Coutts interview (which I never really wanted to take part in, and had no chance on God's earth of ever being invited to accept) had a real positive affect on the outcome of the Barclays interview. So thanks dad. Peter, if you are reading this, do let me know if the Coutts thing was what made the difference!

I worked at Barclays for 11 years in various branches across the Midlands and then ultimately in what was known as the Regional Head Office in Birmingham. In Rugby it was all about banking basics, customer enquiries, preparing bank statements (in those days customer cheques were returned to them with their bank statements as, in case you didn't know, the cheques once cashed or paid in would return to the host branch – its all very different today). But three days in I was summoned, with a young man who had joined the previous year, Steve Brough, to represent the Midlands Region at cricket at Radbroke Hall in Knutsford. Steve was an excellent cricketer. I had come across him when playing for my cricket club Oakfield in Rugby and he was easily a full division ahead of me in terms of cricketing ability, and a really good bloke to boot.

I thought this was great, three days at work and a day off to play cricket. I may have underestimated how my machine room colleagues felt about this and I found myself with a few bridges to build as they probably felt the opposite reaction to me "three days in and he's off playing cricket and we're doing his work!" It was a good match and I got to open the bowling (though batting was where I would have said I was stronger) and took a couple of early wickets. I didn't often get the ball to swing, or if I did, get it to pitch up enough to work, but on this occasion it seemed to work in my favour and I tempted both openers to drive and edge the ball to a hungry group of slips (I wasn't used to slips in my team at Oakfield taking chances regularly, but these lads gobbled them up!)

45

I heard the captain, Brian Jones, who was based at Bilston branch telling one of the other lads in a broad Black Country accent that I had only started at the bank on Monday.

So feeling quite pleased with myself I went on to gain acceptance by the mainly female team who were also working in the machine room (even after the absence through cricket). After I learnt how to avoid blushing every time one of the girls spoke to me or when the phone rang (and I was expected to answer it) found myself enjoying a fairly comfortable experience.

I had been working at the branch in Rugby for 6 weeks when the Coventry away game arrived. I had waited patiently and my friend Mark Williams, also a Stoke fan, was up for the game that we travelled to on my Honda. We parked at the railway station hoping to meet up with hoards of Stoke fans enroute to the match and a large Special Train eventually arrived discharging its contents, a large and rowdy group of Stoke fans. We were given a police escort to the ground. Highfield Road was a good walk from the station and away fans were now situated on a part of the open terrace at the opposite end of the ground to where I had been previously. I remember it as a good match during which Jimmy Hill took some heavy stick. We went 2 – 0 up early in the game, first through an own goal and the second by a rising star in our ranks, Adrian Heath. They pulled one back in the second half, but Garth Crooks scored a third after a break away and we were in the clear. I really enjoyed this one.

I had failed my first round at banking exams (ACIB) despite having enjoyed the luxury of a half day a week study leave, through not doing enough work, plain and simple. This wasn't received well. Over the next few years I performed a range of junior roles at the branch, standing orders, counter, foreign till, personal banker and then progressed into what is known as the securities team whose

46

main role was to put in place any security for lending which the Branch Managers had committed. This could be a charge over property, shares, life policies or personal guarantees. Quite interesting stuff.

I was getting on fairly well, just like Stoke who stayed in the top league for five seasons. Our best finish was 11th in this period in the 1980/81 season where Lee Chapman top scored with fifteen goals. The highlights for me were a home draw against Liverpool where we twice came from behind including a late injury time equalizer by Paul Randall, who slammed the ball in from close range after a scramble to set up some of the most memorable Boothen End scenes I can remember. Kenny Dalglish scored for Liverpool in that game. We also earned a 2 – 2 draw at Coventry toward the end of the season having been 2 – 0 down at half time. Chapman and Paul McGuire from a penalty were our goal scorers and in my records I noted that Peter Fox had a great game.

By the end of the 1980/81 season I was driving having passed my test in March and after a brief affair with a purple Triumph Spitfire, settled down with a bright red Ford Escort. I was up and running.

I was being encouraged to seek broader experience and accept that the world didn't just extend to Barclays Bank in Rugby. At Barclays this almost always meant a transfer to a different branch, often with a promotion, which meant you could just about break even on the additional travel costs. The pack drill was that if you were called into the manager's office on a Thursday afternoon, it usually meant you were on your way on the following Monday. So it proved and with it my opportunity to explore further wonders of the world. Nuneaton.

While at Nuneaton we escaped relegation in the 1983/84 season with an amazing victory on the final day at home to Wolves where

47

Paul McGuire scored all four. My other abiding memory is watching Alan Hudson play for us again (after his return from Arsenal), against Arsenal where he single handedly orchestrated a 1 – 0 victory. I was watching from the Boothen Paddock, close to the pitch and was captivated by his touch and his short five or ten yard passes, the intricate dummies he sold and his simple vision. Alan kept it very simple, but so brilliant and in the twilight of his career I had gotten to glimpse it again at his magical best.

Unfortunately, there would be no escape from relegation the following season and we were resoundingly relegated. I referred to this season in Chapter Five and suffice to say that with just three wins all season and just 17 points gained, we broke quite a few unwanted records that year.

From Nuneaton I moved in the same fashion to Shirley, Solihull. I have only ever been back to Nuneaton once, an occasion I doubt will ever be erased from my memory banks as they knocked us out of the FA Cup. After a 0 - 0 draw at the Victoria Ground, we lost 1 – 0 in the replay in a desperate display in the First Round of the FA Cup in 2000. After a couple of years I was on the move again, this time to Coleshill, a tiny place but where I got on famously. It didn't last long as I was spotted for a promotion and moved to Bedworth, near neighbours of Nuneaton.

Work was going well at Bedworth and I had even passed my exams by this stage and was beginning to realise that there was the chance of a sensible career going on here.

I was getting on well with the new Branch Manager, David Bradley who was far more dynamic than any previous manager I had worked for. He gave me the confidence to really kick start my career and guided me to accept a sideways move to the Birmingham Local Head Office. That opened up a whole new chapter for me. I was living in Birmingham at the time and was well acquainted with the fairly local balti curry scene and was a regular at several brilliant curry house venues in the Sparkbrook area. These were very different to what I had experienced previously; no table cloths or cutlery but family sized naan breads three feet in diameter and basically all you could eat for a fiver. My favourite starter had become *chops-tikka* at *Imrans*, where you received a generous portion of three lamb chops burnt at the edges and crisp and succulent. I was also really impressed by the *Gulab Jamun* desert, especially in the *Royal Al'Faisal*. This was like small balls of syrup sponge, fabulous! The restaurants were unlicensed, but that was fine, the same proprietors owned a neighbouring off license!

Life was busy, I was living with my girlfriend, Yvonne and her daughter Simone who attended many matches with me, (twenty five in all) including Leeds away where we lost 4 – 0, naturally I had chosen to go to this game rather than the home game where we thrashed Leeds 6 – 2.

We finished tenth in Division 2 in this our first season out of the top flight for 5 years and followed that up with eighth in 1986/7, where we beat Leeds 7 – 2 (I missed that game as well) and Grimsby 6 – 0 in the second FA Cup replay (I had chosen the first replay to attend that finished 1 – 1). I did however witness the demolition of Sheffield United 5 – 2 where Carl Saunders scored the first hat trick I had ever seen a Stoke player achieve. So we had new heroes now, yes Carl "Spider" Saunders was one of those, but the Centre Half pairing of no nonsense George Berry and our own Steve Bould really pleased me. George, was also showing his prowess as an accomplished penalty taker. Five of his eight goals were from penalties and he was acquiring cult status. We love our Centre Halves at Stoke.

Steve Bould was a real football player, strong and tough in the challenge but also he possessed genuine football talent. He graced his hometown club's Victoria Ground for seven seasons before earning a £390,000 transfer to Arsenal on thirteenth June 1988, choosing them rather than Everton. It was a great decision for him, and while it was a wrench to see such an accomplished player leave our club, I don't know a Stoke City fan who isn't proud of him and his massive achievements and silverware. He was only absent from Arsenal for two years after a move to Sunderland, where he only played a handful of times before returning to Arsenal as a coach after retiring from playing in 2000. He is currently Arsenal's Assistant Manager. Good luck to you Bouldy, but don't expect any favours when you visit Stoke!

As for George Berry, well he was a brute, and I mean it in a good way. He was tough tackling and never shirked a physical battle, he sported a big afro hairstyle and after joining our club from Wolves in 1982, spent 8 years at Stoke and was a big fans favourite. I don't know why he started to take our penalties, I think after we had missed a couple and he was the skipper so took responsibility. What struck me is not only how hard he smacked the ball each time, but his placement and I am sure that helped him deceive many goalkeepers with his spot kicks. He scored thirty goals in two hundred and sixty nine appearances, that's a better ratio than some of our strikers have recorded. George was a cult hero and unlike some players, really appreciated it. He regards himself as a Stokie and at his testimonial match against Port Vale spent the second half in the Boothen End with his adoring fans after playing his last action at the Victoria Ground in the first half of the game. We didn't get close to winning anything in those eight years but George brightened them up. I also liked his centre half pairing with Noel Blake, who was even scarier than George on the pitch. Oooh Georgie Berry!

I joined the Advances team at Local Head Office, 63 Colmore Row, Birmingham in the Summer of 1986, following the usual pack drill of a Thursday afternoon chat with the Branch Manager and then a Monday morning start in the new job. I was an Advances Clerk, recognized as quite a notable position for its relative lowly grade, which basically meant I was the gofer for one of the Risk Management Directors in Local Head Office, Colmore Row. A great learning and development position without much in the way of additional financial reward. This Local Head Office covered a huge patch, from Rugby in the South to Stoke on Trent in the North of the Midlands.

The Advances team comprised around eight Analysts like me and a Senior Advances Clerk, all still relatively junior, but where high potential was honed. The Directors all had their peculiarities and of course were given nicknames by the Advances team, Peter Monaghan was my favourite, fair, sharp as a dye and funny. Roger Billingham (the Bear) was rude, grisly and always snarling. He was very bear like, pretty fat and overweight. He wasn't a nice bloke. Roger Mellin was the Ghost, he barely looked alive, almost see through and Roger Morgan was the Prism, slightly more than two faced we all felt. Wendy Gadd supplied the glamour, but please don't read too much into that, the vision you now have is sadly wrong. Her nickname was the Bitch, and only Mike Twigger, a colleague of mine could sweet talk her round.

This is where I met Ade, a fellow Stokie who had joined the advances team a few months earlier, and from day one, we clicked and took every opportunity to attend matches anywhere and everywhere. Ade was part of an existing group of lads who used to meet in Uncle Tom's Cabin very near the Victoria Ground, and I was invited to tag along, and since 1986, for the last 30 years and counting, that's what I have done.

It's fair to say that it was quite hierarchical within the Bank and the Advances team survived on its solidarity and humour. Our boss

51

was Mike Priddy, a West Brom fan who came with us to the 6 - 0 thrashing that I have already mentioned. The team was constantly changing as the Advances team was seen as the vehicle through which High Fliers would progress to more senior positions within the bank, especially those on the Management Development Programme (MDP). Ade was one of these.

The general pattern was to parachute these guys and girls into the team, and hope they found their feet fast. It was fast moving and unforgiving, Ade was fine and as a banker like myself (rather than graduates, the usual MDP fare who didn't know the first thing about how branch banking operated). A year or so later, Ade moved to Liverpool to expand his experience and in his place came Dave Mullins. Dave was a graduate and despite being loud, large, almost devoid of common sense, no idea about banking whatsoever he could talk for England. He became my best mate. Dave had the most dreadful collection of casual shirts, truly nauseous, which he took delight is exhibiting at social events. Dave was a good cricketer, not as good as he thought, but good enough. He had a quick delivery when he put his already creaking back into his bowling and nearly took my head off in some outdoor nets at our cricket club on one occasion. He likes beer, lots of it so we had a few things in common from the off.

I went to many matches with Dave over the years including the Autoglass Trophy final versus Stockport where Steino lit up the occasion in a half empty Wembley Stadium as Stockport County, our opponents couldn't sell more than a fraction of their tickets while we shifted more than 40,000. We didn't have the bragging rights however as they had knocked us out of the play-offs a few weeks earlier. Over this two legged affair, Kevin Francis scored very early on at the Victoria Ground to deny us at home after we had lost the away leg 1 – 0.

So the Autoglass was a crumb of comfort that gave us a great day out in the sun and a trophy to boot. Stockport returned to Wembley the week later in the Play off final only to lose that game also, tough luck lads, and they now reside in non league football. One good thing about their demise and ultimately relegation from the football league is that it was one of the very few away grounds across England & Wales I hadn't visited, so them falling out of the league didn't mean it was a ground lost from my 92 Club list.

At the other end of the spectrum Dave was with me and a few others at Plainmoor, Torquay on my first stag do. Poor game which we lost 1 – 0. Messy.

Dave is now occupying a fairly senior position at National Australia Bank in Sydney where he lives with his wife, Jo (also a member of the Advances team in Birmingham) and their daughter Gracie. All being well, by the time you are reading this, I will be at Dave's house in Sydney over New Year 2017/18 and ready for the final test match which commences on 4th January 2018 in Sydney. Hopefully we can also catch a screening of a live Stoke Premier League match at some ungodly hour of the morning in a bar with some other Stokies.

The MDP recruits enjoyed some exotic placements, Dave was posted in Hong Kong for a year and Jo was posted to Gibraltar. I made visits to both with my partner Louise.

The team kept on changing and a number of very likeable guys were coming through, Ian Greatrex and Adrian Ash joined and both very capable guys, who followed me to Nationwide after a few more years.

Barclays soon did the honourable thing and began their five-year sponsorship of the English football leagues in 1987. This was good news as there were possibilities to get hold of tickets to various games, accessing the Directors' Box. The deal meant that the most local larger Barclays branches received 6 tickets to each home league and cup game. A great idea in principle, but one that was either really popular and massively oversubscribed, or at the other end of the spectrum, totally useless as tickets to watch Stoke away at Cambridge United in midweek in February were hard to give away – I did my bit to help out naturally.

Having established a good relationship with the local ticket coordinator at Barclays in Stoke, I was able to take full advantage. We would speak regularly and I would always help her out if she was left with unwanted tickets. However my main interest was getting hold of tickets for away matches and that required a bit more planning and some good reasons why I was deserving of tickets. Being in the Advances Department definitely helped as Branch Managers across the region relied on the Advances team to present their applications to the Local Risk Directors in preferably a positive way, so I usually received a fair hearing.

As the 1980's drew to a close we were treated by the capture of Peter Beagrie, who was a great winger. The problem with him was that he liked to beat a defender not just once, but at least twice and often three times before he got his cross over. Strikers just never knew when he was going to deliver the cross, but he was great to watch and scored some fabulous goals in his fifty four games at Stoke. I recall when he was sold to Everton for £750,000 in 1989, we were rock bottom of Division two and it looked like good business as he had only cost £210,000 from Sheffield United. I saw it differently and in selling your best asset on the pitch, it wasn't going to be easy for the team to succeed.

As Stoke City were banked by Barclays I saw the report from the branch arrive in the Advances Department, referring to the sale of

Beagrie and how this would enable a reduction in the overdraft which had become quite a solid layer of debt. My job was to summarize the report from the branch and add my own recommendation, which the Local Director would consider when making their formal response. To the credit of the Director, Bob Hobday, he included my concerns about the club selling the family silver and what potential impact this might have on future results. So at least I got to raise my points. In the end though, the sale was concluded.

A little earlier in the Spring of 1988 we received the report requesting additional funding to finance the new Executive Boxes at the Victoria Ground. Those familiar with the Ground will know that these were constructed at the back of the Butler Street stand. However there were a number of options in the feasibility study such as locating the boxes low down in the Boothen Stand Paddock. Another option was to use the vacant corner between the Boothen End and Butler Street stand. The right decision was made, approved at Local Head Office (with my recommendation to do so) and at a total construction cost of £260,000, excluding furniture and fittings, the twenty five new boxes opened at the start of the 1989/90 season at home to West Ham. I still have the feasibility report which contains some great photos of the old Victoria Ground, which from time to time I still miss incredibly.

Still in 1988/89 season, Ade and I had our sights set on Hull City away and a good opportunity to exercise my influencing skills to obtain tickets through the sponsorship. I got hold of three tickets and invited an ex colleague, Pete Markham, who I worked with at Bedworth and who now lived in Hull. Ade drove and we met in a traditional boozer in Hull by the docks called the Green Bricks and enjoyed a couple of beers and lunch before heading to Boothferry Park, another new ground to tick off my list.

There was a relative small crowd of 5,915 with my records suggesting around 650 away fans. That excluded us three of course as we were in the Hospitality Room and in Directors' Box seats, I still have the tickets and programme. The Directors' Box at Hull really just meant wooden seats on the half way line, with access to a small room and bar. We may have let ourselves down a bit celebrating in this home area as we scored each goal and continued our celebrations in the lounge and bar after a stunning 4 – 1 win, Carl Beeston got two, Gary Hackett and Nicky Morgan adding the others, all scored in the first half. Billy Whitehurst scored a consolation from 30 yards for the hosts late on, but this didn't take the shine off our day.

The trip home was a good one, always the same after a good win and we noticed the players' coach up ahead (we had stayed behind for a beer to celebrate the result). This was in the era of inflatable's, Man City had bananas, and we had pink panthers, I don't know why, but it introduced some fun. Ade had a giant size inflatable pink panther, fully eight times the usual size and as we passed the team coach the panther was hoisted through the sun-roof for the players to see. They approved and our job was done.

Back at work, Ade and I continued to get on well and though it was a high pressure environment with the morning sessions often becoming quite tense. This depended on the mood of the Directors, who sometimes could never be satisfied. They depended on and leant heavily on the Advances Clerks and it was rewarding but hard graft. The initial exchanges were a catalyst for the rest of the day. First thing in the morning we would carry up to two dozen thick and heavy files to the Directors' floor and wait to be summoned. The Director would then go through each file and the recommendation being made. Some would be requesting additional funding, others about their latest management information, and others reporting that overdraft limit was exceeded which needed to be ratified.

A good result was where the Director used the "*Sanctioned on the Basis of Submitted stamp*" and signed the request off. This wasn't common and mainly they would request analysis on the request which would become our work in progress for the day. Everyone knew how each other had done by the quantity of files that we carried back to our desks to perform the work on.

The mood was lightened later in the morning as the tea trolley arrived, a trolley of industrial scale featuring large steel teapots and china cups and saucers for everyone. For sometime there had been a competition to perform the fastest tea run, getting everyone their particular drink, with correct milk and sugar requirements. It didn't happen every day, but occasionally when the workload was just a bit lighter, a pair of colleagues would compete to break the time record. I can't remember precisely when we did it, but Ade and I took on the challenge one morning, it was organized chaos as we charged around the desks and delivered everyone's specified drink, we knew we had a good chance provided we hadn't mucked up the orders or lost a cup and saucer enroute. The verdict arrived shortly afterwards and he and I became the proud record holders, smashing the previous record.

The Advances team remained at 63 Colmore Row for a couple more years before moving to smaller but neater office space where we were sensibly located on the same floor as the Directors, but while that made sense it saw the end of the timed tea and coffee runs. Our record remained intact.

While planning for the tea run challenge, we were eagerly awaiting our next away game at Maine Road, Man City and the plan was for everyone to be in fancy dress, we all went in old school uniform style and had our panthers, including the beast. This was a big away following and the display of fancy dress and panthers was a sight to behold in the away stand behind the goal. We actually played

57

well, but still found ourselves 2 – 0 down before John Butler's goal gave us a lifeline near the end. I estimated 5,000 away fans at that game and while it didn't quite happen for us, it was a good day and another ground off my list.

My final away game of this season was at Bournemouth and this time on the occasion of Ade's stag do, a sunny day by the sea on 15th April 1989. This ended up being quite a strange day. We won having been totally outplayed and near the end Paul Ware swung a hopeful cross into their box, with no Stoke players in sight, their keeper inexplicably fumbled the cross under no pressure and bundled it into his own net. We took it and celebrated among the small group of away fans. Toward the end of the game, news was filtering through about the Hillsborough disaster and while we had no idea of the scale of this, it was becoming clear that this was a catastrophe.

The night followed standard stag do format and we had found a hotel which agreed to accept us and which must have been close to being condemned. The all in price was £10 each including breakfast. While the boys continued their party and were driving to Dover to cross the channel for another night, I took the train home as I was studying for some Advanced Level Bank exams. After struggling at CSE level, at College and with my early bank exams it was as though a switch had been flicked and I was enjoying the work and passing the exams.

One final game to mention in that season, at home to Leeds United, on the last day of the season, two highlights to report, first Dave Bamber scored twice (and that's not something often said about him at Stoke) and second, Leeds scored their winner in the second half through an audacious chip from the corner of the box by Gordon Strachan. I don't like Leeds and I don't like Strachan, but his goal was simply brilliant.

The 1989/90 season did start with optimism, Ian Cranson joined for a record fee of £480,000 and Wayne "Bertie" Biggins was also signed up and he definitely had a bit of class as a striker. He scored in the opening game at home to West Ham in a 1 – 1 draw and spirits were good. Port Vale were now in the same league having achieved promotion over Bristol Rovers in the two legged play off final, in the days where the final was not played at Wembley.

Our first away day of this season was at Wolves, where we had snared all six of the Barclays tickets which were in the main stand. Games at Wolves are always a bit edgy and this one was no different. We took our seats, probably knowing that we wouldn't get away with the celebrations that Ade and I enjoyed at Hull. We played really well and dominated the game. Toward the end of the first half we got a penalty and there was noticeably some trouble not far behind us as some Stoke fans celebrated that decision. That gave us time to consider how we might respond to scoring the penalty and while it was volatile in there, there was no way all six of us could have sat on our hands had a goal been scored. However, Derek Statham let us off the hook by missing the penalty, and while this was really irritating, it might have saved our skins. The game finished 0 – 0 and we had quite a lot to be positive about.

Alan Ball had arrived at the club as assistant to Mick Mills in October 1989, by which time we had not won in our first eleven games. Mick Mills was then sacked and after only two weeks at the club, Ball was appointed as Manager. It was a popular decision at the time and we all felt that he couldn't do any worse that Mills. We were wrong. His managerial record at Stoke was awful and while the fans stayed with him, his explanations of results and the decisions he was making were really poor. We were relegated that season to Division Three for the first time in sixty three years.

Despite the team's form and all the negativity, we continued to enjoy our excursions and another new ground was on the horizon, Blackburn away. Despite a 3 - 0 reverse which could have been more but for great goalkeeping and a penalty save by Peter Fox, Stoke fans kept up the singing of "Alan Ball's red and white army" for a whole half of the game.

In February we achieved a rare win against Staffordshire rivals Wolves at home. It gave us false hope. I had driven with a colleague John Hyde, a Wolves fan happy to experience the Boothen End with me. Biggins scored our opener, the last action I saw as in the riotous celebration my glasses flew off and were trampled. Both lenses smashed. We won 2 – 0 and John had to drive my car home.

I attended more games in this season than I had ever been able to previously, twenty seven in total, and after being accepted into Ade's group, met religiously at Uncle Tom's for home games and stood near the back of the Boothen End with the lads. This was a different spot to that which I had been using when going to games on my own which was the terrace area immediately at the top of the stairs into the Boothen End right behind the goal. It was an area that was always jammed. It was also still very busy up on the next layer where Ade and the guys stood and we always found our spot together.

And so as I became a much more regular visitor at matches, the club were relegated to the Third Division. Amazingly spirits were high and none more so than at the final away game of the season at Brighton which was the cue for an invasion of Brighton and at the end we flooded on to the pitch to celebrate a thrilling 4 – 1 win before heading to the beach where festivities continued. We had all gone in Hawaiian style beach wear and the beast of a pink panther was centre stage on Ade's shoulders. Biggins scored and Tony "Elvis" Ellis got two.

As the MDP cohorts came and left, I began to realize how good

60

the experience and training had been. Since Black Monday in October 1987, resulting from a stock exchange collapse of unprecedented size, a global slowdown was underway. It took longer to affect the UK and it was 1990 before a Recession was officially called. Interest rates and inflation were sky high. Base rate was over 14% in 1990 and the affect this had on mortgage payments led to a major fall in house prices.

Commercial Property had also been hit hard by falling values and in particular, was in a serious downturn. I was working directly for the *Bear* and while that was an opportunity to learn a lot, was a tough shift. One of my colleagues, Ian, had applied and got an interview at Nationwide in Northampton at their huge Administration Centre in the out of town Moulton Park site.

Ian was offered a job, but declined that initial opportunity. This took my interest and I applied for a more senior role on almost double the money that I was currently on, the equivalent of at least two promotions within the Bank and probably another three to five years hard graft. I was offered the role after a day of interviews and testing. It just seemed right and I took the plunge and after eleven enjoyable years I left Barclays and joined Nationwide in 1990

CHAPTER EIGHT
Recession, early Nationwide
years and arrival of the Messiah
1990/93

Economic recession and crisis within the banking industry go hand in hand, history proves this and Barclays had pulled out of Commercial Property lending before I left the bank in Autumn 1990. It was an astute decision. Many other banks and building societies saw this kind of lending, more commonly known as Real Estate Finance, as a way to generate additional income over and above highly competitive and commoditised retail products such as mortgage, savings and personal banking accounts.

Nationwide Anglia was a product of the merger of Nationwide and Anglia Building Societies in 1987. They had got themselves into a number or Commercial Property deals toward the top of the market by using a retail mortgage lending product for Commercial Property borrowers. This was nowhere near comprehensive enough to be able to identify risks in this Real Estate sector nor provide the triggers and levers to be able to take control and, hopefully, stabilize situations and enable the Society to get its money back.

Property Investors looking to borrow took full advantage. They lapped up the lending with very few of the types of covenant normally expected in this market, taking advantage of the generous terms including high levels of loan to value. This meant that the investor's personal stake, (their equity) was relatively small in comparison to the debt element. If prices soared investors would take all the capital profit and if they crashed, which happened in this recession, they only stood to lose their modest stake. The Society, just like many other lenders in this sector, was left with a range of part completed sites, horrible portfolios in need of investment, and (more by luck than judgment) a number of actually quite good relationships which they nursed to health and where customers remain on the books through to this day.

Where some of these borrowers were experiencing really hard times on the projects, it would be commonplace for them to hand the keys in to the Lender, leaving them to clear up the mess and try and get at least some of their money back. More often than not there was no recourse to the borrowers personally. Not a great situation which continued to worsen for several years, improvement only beginning to show in 1996. House prices suffered badly with a fall of over 35% on average across the UK. Many of the borrowers were engaged in forms of house building and development. This all came to a very sharp stop.

The Society saw some of this coming and engaged some experienced personnel with a Real Estate background to help control the situation. This was where I came in, though my experience until this point was largely on the technical side, making sure the lending was in line with reasonable policy and terms and conditions for the sector. This was urgently needed to get a handle on the problem which was snowballing.

Every day files would turn up from building society branches across the UK where the managers had engaged in this lending without being in a position to fully understand the risks. Neither was there an effective underwriting function that could weed out the really dodgy opportunities from those that just needed some restructuring to make them into pretty sensible deals.

I was very grateful for the opportunity to accept a more senior role and ultimately stayed at the Society for 18 years in a variety of roles, which was, for the most part, a hugely enjoyable challenge, working with good and like minded people.

Just weeks before I began work at Nationwide, Stoke started their first season in the Third Division for 63 years with a good win against Rotherham on 25th August 1990. We won 3 – 1 at home where Micky Thomas who had been re-signed was on the score sheet. Our second game was away at Tranmere. I had joined Ade who was now working for Barclays in Liverpool, for the match. We won again with Ellis on target with a glancing header then a Mick Kennedy penalty, 2 – 1 and we were top!

It was all quite short lived however and by the time we travelled to Grimsby, enjoying the hospitality of the Barclays tickets as the away allocation had sold out. The cracks in our side were visible. Because we were enjoying some hospitality, Ade took his fiancé Dawn and I took my partner Louise and her sister Alison (who lives in Hull). The main stand at Grimsby is quite impressive, the other three stands are not. The large away support was to our right packing out the terrace. To their left between them and the main stand was a popular, and on this sunny day, very busy family section for away fans with younger children who might actually want to see some of the game. It didn't work out well, Grimsby scored twice in the second half to secure a 2 – 0 win and in truth, we were well beaten.

Before retiring to the lounge for a drink which we all felt was needed a number of quite lively Grimsby fans had invaded the pitch and were making their way toward the away support. It started to get quite nasty. The main block of Stoke fans were hemmed in behind a fence and high fronted iron gate, though they were trying furiously to escape and confront the hundred of so Grimsby fans on the pitch. Meanwhile, the Grimsby fans turned their attention to the Stoke fans occupying the family terrace as there was no fencing fronting this area. This drove the main block of Stoke fans wild as they saw families being attacked. From the front of the upper tier of the main stand we also vented our feelings. Before long the gate could withstand no more and several hundred Stoke fans entered the fray, this led to a rapid retreat by the home fans who, quite satisfyingly were getting some of their own medicine. My notes suggest it was the worst crowd trouble I had witnessed, unfortunately it wasn't a record that was to last very long.

Alan Ball was sacked in February after a 4 – 0 humbling at the hands of Wigan. I was upset with Alan Ball and his mismanagement of a squad that should have been doing so much better. I met him on a trip to Chicago in 2005, fifteen years later and we made our peace over a large Glenmorangie in the quiet hotel bar. The 1990/91 season ended with the club 14th in Division Three, the lowest ever finish for the club.

I was enjoying life and work at Nationwide where I had a good level of discretion to visit customers and help sort out problems and consider new commercial lending opportunities. I had my first ever company car, a Vauxhall Astra which could really shift and I was already sussing out where I could combine customer visits with midweek away matches. I was living back in Rugby now, so slightly longer journeys to home games.

Lou Macari arrived in the Summer, the Messiah, even though we didn't know it yet. The arrivals of Vince Overson (I told you we liked our tough centre halves) and Mark Stein gave the squad further depth and a potent attacking force. Vince cost £55,000 a real steal and Steino was £100,000, just the most incredible piece of business. Between Biggins and Stein they scored fifty goals, Biggins with twenty eight and Stein twenty two. There were many highlights in this season of transformation that restored pride and belief in what our club could achieve.

The League Cup games against Liverpool stick out as a highlight where an army of 8,000 went to support the lads in a memorable game at Anfield that finished 2 – 2. We twice equalized through a powerful Cranson header and then went completely mental when Tony Kelly raced one on one with Bruce Grobbelaar in the final minute before rolling the ball through his legs and slowly into the net. At this game the excitement was such that both Louise and Dawn didn't need much persuading to join us and also Simon, another member of our group who was a good look a like of Bruce Grobbelaar in the Liverpool goal. Simon's wife Karen also joined us.

The question now was, could we finish it in the second leg at home. I was joined on this trip by a couple of colleagues from Nationwide, Martin O'Reilly and also Ian Greatrex. Ian who had followed me to Nationwide from Barclays. After a quick beer in a rammed Uncle Tom's Cabin, we were in the Boothen End on time and slowly edged our way to the usual spot. We went 1 – 0 down quite early on, then early in the second half the unfortunate Tony Kelly rolled a back pass straight into Dean Saunders path and he scored easily. Now we were well under the cosh. In the second half we rallied and after sustained pressure were awarded a penalty after intentional handball on the line. Biggins rammed the ball home but my question was why no sending off? It was then end to end and Liverpool scored a third after a well executed counter attack. We weren't finished though as Biggins had time to head in from close range beating Grobbelaar to the high ball. A brave effort.

I remained a regular at home games, and was still accessing tickets from Barclays to some away games where match tickets were hard to get hold of in the away section. This included Exeter, where Alan Ball was now managing and where an incident with a cup of tea being thrown at him took place. The game ended 0 – 0. The bank tickets also came in handy at Hull again, where we managed a 1 – 0 win this time with Kevin "Rooster" Russell on the score sheet. I was attending lots of other away games too and our followings were getting larger and larger. The game at West Brom finished 2 – 2 where Vince Overson scored twice. This was our fifth game against West Brom since the 6 – 0 hammering and little did we know that it was only the beginning of a very long unbeaten run against the Baggies.

We had not been the only "bigger" club to suffer relegation to the third division. West Brom had joined us along with Birmingham City and we were all close Midlands rivals. By the time we played Birmingham City away on 29th February 1992, we together with West Brom and Birmingham were all fighting for the automatic promotion places. This led to a very large crowd at St Andrews and I was with two mates who were colleagues at Nationwide, Adrian Ash and Jeremy Allcock (a Blues fan on his 7th formal birthday – he was born on 29th February and was 28 years old) and arrived in the ground at 14.50 just before kick off. It was packed on the away terrace and I beckoned the lads nearer to the front of the terrace. Despite my honed techniques of moving through people in the crowd, this was never going to work as it was already so full, so we went a bit further back and edged our way into a spot.

It was a lively affair and Birmingham were certainly up for it. They took a deserved lead in the first half and we were hanging on a bit. The atmosphere was good but you could tell it had a nasty side to it, from both sets of supporters. As we approached the latter stages we had increased the pressure and were pushing for an equalizer. With just a few minutes to go a long hopeful ball was pumped up toward Wayne Biggins, but their keeper was favourite to reach it and seemed to. Wayne followed through and it looked like a nasty collision which injured the keeper. The ball however had squirmed away from the keeper and while Wayne was also still on the floor removing his studs from the keepers groin, there was Paul Barnes all alone and with an empty net. He, like me and probably everyone else in the ground had expected to hear the whistle, there was none, so after a brief look around he casually rolled the ball in and it was 1 – 1. The celebrations on the away terrace reached new heights and were riotous. You can imagine the reaction of the Blues fans in the nearby pen and its fair to say that Stoke fans did their best to rub this in.

Reviews of the game suggest that it was this late equalizer that prompted the pitch invasion which occurred shortly afterwards, but I don't think so. My recollection was that immediately after the restart Birmingham had an amazing chance to retake the lead. Somehow in the scramble that ensued the ball, which looked as if it had crossed the line, was cleared. No goal. And at that point it happened, they came from all four sides of the ground, from the Kop, a terrace spanning the full length of the pitch and where the bulk of home fans congregate, from the adjacent pen behind the goal, from the Main stand to our right which featured two tier seating and also from the other end of the ground, the old Railway Stand (which now houses away fans). This wasn't a few upset idiots, this was orchestrated and literally thousands congregated on the pitch, many of whom approached the front of our away terrace and tried to access in large numbers.

The police did their best, but I recall the few dozen Stoke fans who lined the fence were like gladiators and fought furiously with the invaders. The battle took place along the perimeter fence, very near where I had encouraged my friends to stand but couldn't find a space. We remain in the debt of those Stoke fans and it is a day I will never forget. The players had been taken off and the game abandoned for all we knew, in fact that's what was announced to help clear the stadium.

68

We got back to our car safely, colours hidden. But a young Stoke fan also heading away from the match lost an eye in the exchanges where missiles were thrown. It was the worst trouble I had ever seen, eclipsing the skirmishes at Grimsby.

The players did return to the field later to play out the remaining sixty seconds or so and 1 – 1 was the final score.

The season ended with us in the Playoffs rather than the automatic promotion we had craved. Brentford won the league and Birmingham took the second automatic promotion place. We finished in 4th place facing Stockport County in the two legged play off semi final. We lost the first away leg 1 – 0 and it was all on the home game now. Early on our hopes took a serious blow as the gangly Kevin Francis scored in the first few minutes. We recovered to 1 – 1, Steino naturally, but couldn't force the winner and that particular Wembley and promotion dream was over.

During that season we also played eight games in the Autoglass Trophy, a competition for Division Three and Four teams, culminating with an appearance at Wembley. I saw us win comfortably at Walsall 2 – 0, Lee Sandford netting twice, beat Birmingham and Cardiff and then on to Leyton Orient where I travelled down to London and met Dave Mullins to see the match. Steino scored from a sharp shot in off the post and we were in the semi finals against Peterborough.

The semi final was a two leg affair, and the first leg was at home. We raced into a two goal lead with Biggins getting both and then collapsed to a 3 – 2 deficit, before grabbing a late equalizer to at least keep us on level terms. I had got my ticket for the second leg at London Road and along with 4000 others headed east. This was a relatively short trip for me and I entered the traditional style and packed away terrace on a cold sharp April night. We played really

69

well. It was a game that could take us to Wembley for the first time since 1972 and with ten or fifteen minutes remaining we were awarded a free kick about twenty five yards out. We were a bit surprised to see Paul Ware teeing the ball up, he also had an arm in plaster during the game and unleashed a cracker which simply flew in at the away end, delirium.

I wasn't nervous at all at the final, I had met Ade and the lads and Dave and Jo at a great real ale pub in St Johns Wood and after a few drinks, enjoyed the tube trip to Wembley where at each stop more and more Stoke fans boarded. The atmosphere was fabulous and the walk up Wembley Way a feeling that Stoke fans had yearned for decades. The win, courtesy of a great rising shot from Steino gave us the trophy and the players celebrated with us with a huge Delilah which rung around the stadium, now half empty and containing only Stoke City fans.

At work we were still wrestling with commercial loans in varying condition, many in need of intensive care. I was head of the Commercial Recoveries team by this time, managing these cases and trying to nurse them back to full health or at least minimize the loss to the Society. One of the loans in the portfolio I was looking after was to a company owned by Garry Gibson who had some residential developments in the North East financed by Nationwide. These were becoming problematic. Garry was also the chairman of Hartlepool United, newly promoted, and I would meet him at a match in the new season.

1992/93 was surely going to be the year? We started at Hull and Mr Barclays was still showing generosity with the tickets, even though I had left the bank three years earlier. Again the usual crew including Hull contingent (Pete and Alison) were looking forward to the match. This time we didn't live up to the expectation among the 4,000 travelling fans and lost 1 – 0, but we had played well.

By the time we beat West Brom in a thriller at Home 4 – 3, we were four matches unbeaten. My notes from the West Brom game suggest it's the best game that I had ever seen. The scoring went 0 – 1, 1 – 1, 2 – 1, 2 – 2, 2 – 3, 3 – 3 and finally 4 – 3. "Rooster" Russell got two and Steve Foley and Ian Cranson also found the net.

In the following game away at Mansfield we won so convincingly it was almost embarrassing and at Burnley a double by Graham Shaw saw us seal a great away win. We were on an unbeaten run which would span twenty five league games from 5th September to 20th February. I was there when it began in a dreary draw against Bolton at home, and at Leyton Orient where it came to an end 1 – 0. But we had momentum, we were by far the best team in the league and points continued to flow.

A low point from this season was that Port Vale knocked us out of the FA Cup. This was the game with the Dave Regis "ball stuck in mud as it was rolling into the empty net" incident, to be honest he should have just leathered it. I was behind the goal close to the pitch willing it in, but it wasn't obedient. They also knocked us out of the Autoglass Trophy and while I've never had a beef with them, they were really starting to irritate me. We would get our own back!

After a good away win at Blackpool in the rain where Rooster Russell ran riot, we were heading for Hartlepool. I had booked Louise and I into a hotel in town so that I could meet with Garry Gibson the following morning to discuss his loan facilities and his property developments. He had established radio silence.

Hartlepool is a good ground to get off your list. Its miles from anywhere and if you think Stoke needs a facelift, well Hartlepool is a further few rungs down the ladder. It was very cold and on the 19th December we were meeting Ade and Dawn to stand on the open away terrace in the freezing weather. Dave Regis gave us the lead in the first half but when they equalized it looked like it wasn't to be. Near the end we had a what looked a good headed goal disallowed and then in the final seconds Nigel Gleghorn scored with a fantastic header which soared into the top corner right in front of us. The celebrations kept us warm.

I drove from the hotel to the ground for our meeting the following morning and waited for Gibson. He never showed up. I was furious and wrote to him directly from work on Monday threatening him with a formal demand on his loans unless there was immediate response. Things improved right away, interest was serviced and when I insisted that we reconvene the meeting, he suggested that we do this in Stoke on the day of the Hartlepool game. I accepted, but didn't know what was to come.

In between times we continued our good form and enjoyed a great 2 – 2 draw at Brighton's old Goldstone Ground where a last minute equalizer by Steve Foley kept our run going. Our next away game was at West Brom where a massive crowd for Division Three (29,341) including many thousands of Stoke fans celebrated a hard fought victory. Gleghorn and then Steino got our goals and we sang "you're only ten points behind us" to the tune of *Quanta La Mera*, great fun!

We were now well into March and top of the league. My Commercial Recoveries team were making good strides forward and covered the entire UK from four regional centre's in Manchester in the North, Swindon in the West, Sevenoaks in the South and Northampton in the East Midlands. One of the largest problem cases involved a site of 70 acres in Bristol at Avon Riverside. This was potentially a good site, however Nationwide had financed it on a speculative basis, before planning permission, on the basis that all 70 acres were developable (when in fact less than half were). There was also the issue of contamination, problems with the National Rivers Association and with several protected Badger Sets. As lenders in possession of the site (the owners were bankrupt), we had responsibility for the lot. We had to re-home the badgers at a cost of over £5k!

I coincided a full day visit with Stoke due to play in Swansea that night, it was the penultimate occasion I had relied on using the Barclays tickets and was advised by the local branch to contact the club direct and speak to Hugh, club secretary. He seemed quite accommodating when I phoned him up and said that if I asked for him on arrival at the Vetch Field Ground, he would furnish me with two tickets.

My colleague and mate Dave White, a passionate Northampton Town fan came with me and we did the site visit and meetings during the day – what a mess – then travelled on to Swansea. We parked up a little way from the ground and made our way to the stadium after a beer about an hour before kickoff. I approached reception at the main entrance and referred to my conversation with Hugh and was waved through and upstairs. When I eventually got to speak to him he was incredibly rude and denied all knowledge of the conversation, I was gob smacked.

What could we do? We walked back downstairs, but instead of turning right and leaving through the door we had used to enter, we turned left and within a few seconds we found ourselves on that strange narrow piece of terracing opposite the away end. Very few people were about so we stayed put. We figured that it might be best to ask to move to the away fans terrace at the other end of the ground and a very obliging steward escorted us there. It started to fill up quite quickly as coaches arrived and we got ready to watch the game. The crowd was 8,366 with around 1,500 away fans, I estimated. But you could sense there was something just a little bit odd about the atmosphere.

We were losing 1 – 0 at half time an Andy Legg volley that beat a sprawling Bruce Grobbelaar who was on loan to us. We did play very well in the second half and had several chances, from one of these Steve Foley scored to equalize and while we celebrated as usual, the home fans had got the real hump. It was a Wales v England thing and their reaction to the equalizer seemed a bit over the top. They were on the pitch, climbing the walls etc and we were starting to wonder what our journey would be like back to the car. We continued to press and from a great cross near the end of the game, Nigel Gleghorn arrowed a brilliant header into the very top corner, very similar to his header late on at Hartlepool and we were celebrating again. This didn't help the mood of the locals and at full time they were also trying to scale very high fences to get into the away fans section. Outside it was carnage, police and sirens everywhere, missiles coming over the wall to where the coaches were parked and Dave and I had find the car on foot. We decided to keep our mouths shut as while I have a passable Scottish accent, being half Scottish on my mum's side, my Welsh sounds rather Pakistani.

We found the car safely. There were still various groups of fans giving abuse to the coaches and vans taking Stoke fans out of the town. I spoke to a fellow Stoke fan, also at the game, a few weeks later who said that one van that was being targeted stopped by a roundabout and a group of unsavoury Stoke fans gave a bit back before leaving the town. I don't know if that's true, but I would like to believe it was. I would be tempted to say that at least it's a ground off my list, but of course they have gone and relocated to the purpose built Liberty Stadium so I had to go all over again. I returned this season in 2017 on a lovely sunny day. The reception in Swansea was extremely friendly this time and while we lost 2 – 0, it was a good day out.

This was a memorable season and quite possible to write a book just on this year alone. I have two more matches to give a special mention to, before leaving this momentous year behind. Automatic promotion and the league title were secured in a 1 - 0 win against Plymouth at home in midweek where Peter Shilton graced the Victoria Ground for one final occasion as their goalkeeper and manager.

Prior to the Plymouth game we played Hartlepool at home. I was instructed to wait outside the main stand wearing a shirt and tie to meet Garry Gibson, their Chairman. It was going to be a bit more relaxed as we had sorted out most of the issues on his development schemes. He turned up about 2.30pm and in his broad North East accent told me I was to pretend to be a visiting Director of Hartlepool United. The Directors lounge at Stoke was a very small private room for Club Directors and visiting Directors only, oh and one special guest, Sir Stanley Matthews.

Garry Gibson was a big bloke, 6ft 6ins and broad. He headed straight for the bar, and Sir Stan shook my hand and offered me a programme, he told me his name and that he was looking forward to the match. I was speechless, as if he needed to introduce himself to me, I felt incredibly humble and fortunate to share a short conversation before a Director of Stoke came over and asked me if I thought we (Hartlepool) could stay up, I got by as Garry quaffed gin and tonics with Peter Coates. Garry had some more advice for me before the game started, which was basically not to celebrate like an idiot when Stoke score, "We don't do that type of thing in here", he said. We just had time to go pitch side as Garry wanted to speak to his manager and he introduced him to me. It was Viv Busby, our striker in the early days who I remembered fondly, what a day I was having.

The ground was filling up with a healthy crowd and the few Hartlepool fans were in the corner as most of the Stoke End terrace and seating were being made available to Stoke fans such was the demand. We had chance after chance and eventually a penalty which Mark Stein was about to take. Steino's penalty wasn't good and was saved by their keeper but the rebound came right back to him at a good heading height and incredibly he put the header wide from eight yards and with the keeper on the deck. In the second half it was quite tight, we played as though we were suffering from nerves in trying to secure those final points for promotion and the league title.

Hartlepool seemed to take confidence from this. Late on after a bit of a scramble in our box they only go and score and this is too much for Garry who threw his very large frame around in the Directors Box seating area uncontrollably, the complete opposite to the advice he had given me. It was quite embarrassing. In those days it was apparently customary for the visiting Chairman to receive a slip of paper recording the crowd and match receipts, just for information. When Garry saw this he was very jealous of our club. Knowing he wouldn't be seeing a penny of it, he handed it to me. I still have the slip, it records the crowd of 17,363 and gate receipts for that match of £63,642.50, signed M.J.Potts, Secretary.

Garry asked if I could drop him at Stoke Railway station on my way home and he told me about his plans for the evening and the Sunday. He was apparently going to the Carling Cup Final at Wembley and was in the Royal Box. He asked me to look out for him and his female companion, his lawyer apparently, who he was hoping to get lucky with on the Saturday night. He was supposed to be sitting right behind the dignitaries who were presenting he trophy. I had no real interest in Arsenal's 2 – 1 win over Sheffield

Wednesday (who were to lose again at Wembley that season also against Arsenal in the FA Cup Final, which must have been gutting), but I tuned in at the end and sure enough Garry was there as large as life, un-missable at six foot six, and by the grin he was wearing, maybe he did get lucky.

The last time I managed to access some Barclays tickets was at the final away game at Bolton, naturally I had arranged to coincide a meeting in Manchester with Alan Birkhead who led my Northern recoveries team based in Sale and we fitted in a game of golf on the sunny afternoon before the match. Alan wasn't a footie fan but humoured me and came along. He was a bit perplexed. The reason for that that was that Stoke fans cheered the Bolton goal in a 1 – 0 reverse with vigor and all the fans celebrated together at the end because it meant that Port Vale would miss out on promotion at Bolton's expense. So both Bolton and Stoke fans alike were happy with that and promotion was already secure.

What a season! Champions and back in Division One, Steino had written his name into our history books and we had a very good squad. Lou Macari was indeed the Messiah.

CHAPTER NINE
More Nationwide Years and Back in the Championship

By the start of the 1993/4 season, I had moved into a different part of the Commercial Division at Nationwide and was Head of a small team within the larger Housing Association lending unit. It was all very new to me and I took a while acclimatizing. My team was responsible for the structuring and delivery of funding for what were known as Large Scale Voluntary Transfers (LSVT) of local authority council housing to Housing Associations who had the power to borrow and invest in the properties.

This was to become very big business and I had a 3 day hand over with the ongoing Head of the team, Don, who had a PhD in rat psychology. Don was incredibly bright and clearly knew his stuff. The problem was, I couldn't understand a word of it, it was all double dutch, nothing to do with his relatively soft Scottish accent, just the combination of sets of words I had never heard before and would never be able to spell. We lasted one morning, I went home and rejoined the team when he had left, then it all seemed to make perfect sense!

This was quite a specialist market with only a few lenders involved (at this stage) and so between Nationwide, Halifax and Nat West, we pretty much cornered the market. The average funding requirement was £30m+ and often much larger, so there was plenty to go around.

The 1993/4 season started at home to Milwall and was a bit of a baptism of fire against a side who were seasoned campaigners in this second tier of the game. We lost 2 -1. Lou Macari had strengthened the squad by adding players such as Toddy Orlygsson and Simon Sturridge as well as Goalkeeper, Mark Prudhoe (Russ Abbot look a like).

We settled into some reasonable form, we beat West Brom at home (of course) and won at Middlesborough. Then in the televised game away at Nottingham Forest, we raced into a three goal lead, with Steino scoring the pick of the goals after a back heel from Toddy, with a sumptuous volley. We hung on to win 3 – 2 and next up were Man United at home in the League cup. The United game brought with it great expectation and in one of the most memorable games at the Victoria Ground for many years, we triumphed 2 – 1 in the first leg. First Steino scored from a tight angle when he had no right to do so, with a vicious shot leaving Peter Schmeichel stranded. While Dion Dublin equalized (against the run of play) Steino pounced again with the winner at the Boothen End. A certain Mark Hughes was playing for United that night too. Lou Macari enjoyed this performance against the club he played for so famously.

So we were all set for the away leg at Old Trafford which turned out to be quite one sided and ultimately we were overcome 2 – 0 and our cup run was over. Unfortunately Steino had attracted too much attention and was sold to Chelsea for a record £1.4m, a bid too generous for Stoke to ignore, but this was a blow to the heart. Worse was to follow as Lou Macari, the architect of our revival left the club for his beloved Celtic. We appointed Joe Jordan who was himself manager of Celtic. It was a kind of swap arrangement which was very much in their favour.

Surely Joe, a big centre forward for Leeds and Scotland and a full blooded striker would bring a brand of attacking football to Stoke.

No. Joe's tactics were not the blood and thunder attacking we had hoped for. We ended the season in 10th spot, and the season included some quite interesting games, first a 5 – 4 win against Barnsley (my one and only 5 – 4 game) which I talk about later in the book. Then the weirdest result losing 6 – 2 at Luton, having been 2 – 0 up. Oldham knocked us out of the FA Cup in a replay following a 0 – 0 draw at Boundary Park, and by god it was cold up there. Oldham were a premier league club and defeated us 1 – 0 in the replay where I attended with my Nationwide colleagues as a team night out, stopping in Birmingham for a Balti on the way! We had our chances and Toddy hit the bar early on.

Joe Jordan had introduced Canadian Paul Peschisolido from Birmingham, he had to leave Birmingham as he was in a relationship with their Chief Executive, Karen Brady, so we got a good deal and he was a very useful striker with a low centre of gravity. It always looked as though his shorts were too long. 1994/95 season began with Joe still in charge but there was quite a bit of discontent. We won on the opening day against Tranmere, 1 – 0 with the reliable Gleghorn scoring but then it went down hill fast and after two consecutive 4 – 0 away defeats against Reading and then Bolton, Jordan resigned and Asa Hartford stepped in as caretaker manager. He started well and in a great performance we beat Southend 4 – 1 at home followed by a win over Charlton and a very sound win at Notts County 2 – 0, the first time I had returned to Meadow Lane since the drama of the promotion to Division One in 1979. It's a steep stand that houses the away fans and you get a decent view, this was a good performance.

By the time we played West Brom on 2nd October, the Messiah, Lou Macari had amazingly returned and was warmly welcomed back. Naturally we beat West Brom 4 – 1. We were nicely warmed up for Liverpool away in the cup, hoping we could repeat the heroics of a few years earlier, but unfortunately not this time, though Pesch did score an equalizer to give us hope and the chance to celebrate a goal at Anfield once again.

On 17th January 1995 my daughter, Sarah was born, not into an epic era of Stoke City football unfortunately and though Sarah isn't mad keen on the footie, she does look out for our results while at University in Leeds. She was lovely and I wondered when I would escort her to her first game.

I still managed to attend a handful of games toward the end of the season including the regulation win against West Brom away 3 – 1 where Keith Scott scored (amazingly) and Pesch got two. With Port Vale now also in the division with us, we sadly lost at home to them before winning in style against Millwall 4 – 3 with a very last minute winner. I was with my Nephew Duncan who was about 12 years old and we were heading toward the exit when Kevin Keen bagged the late goal. We were in a bit of a hurry leaving and caught sight of some Millwall fans also driving back South. With a handmade sign which proudly headlined the match score, we set off after them. It took a while, they were shifting, but eventually just North of Birmingham we passed them and caused some mild irritation by displaying our sign. Duncan enjoyed the moment anyway and he had seen a great game for his one and only Stoke City match.

Luton away was the final game of the season and we finished in style with a 3 – 2 win. A late goal from Keith Scott sealed it and we left happy. I remember that Mark Stein was in the ground that day and got a massive welcome from the travelling Stokies. So 11th place, all very steady.

Large Scale Voluntary Transfers – big business!

The world of Housing Association finance was increasing and of growing importance to deliver the level of investment required to create the decent living standards that were by now law. My team had become expert in the funding of these housing transfers and regularly presented to Associations to become their chosen funder. Interesting that I, from a council housing background, would be so involved in the finance of these homes and I found it irritating when people referred to the housing as "Stock" or "Units" when we were talking about people's homes. Anyway, my colleagues and I seemed to strike a chord with this part of the sector and we were achieving some big successes.

These transfers of council housing tended to generate a substantial payment to the local authority, the vendor, averaging around £10,000 per dwelling. This was calculated through a complex cash flow model and took into account all of the initial "catch up" repairs required and the longer term predicted maintenance cost together with the predicted rent levels over a 30 year term. Around two thirds of the rent was met by benefits that the tenants claimed and so in most cases tenants were less affected by rent increases. Our job was to fund the cash flow of the Housing Association acquiring the housing being transferred starting with the capital sum payable to the council. Plus further funding for the catch up repairs (major repairs that had been put off or delayed by the council which could entail new windows, roofing etc). As rents grew (at this point typically by RPI +1% per annum), the Housing Association would begin to repay debt starting at around year ten, with full repayment at 25 or 30 years.

From the lenders perspective this was a good bet as most of the serviceability came through housing benefit and the sector was fully regulated at the time by the Housing Corporation. It was low risk compared to many other commercial lending opportunities and a good fit with Nationwide's UK housing agenda.

We had become the most successful lender to this sector in the UK and as well as underwriting large individual loans of upwards of £100m, we also broke the mould and arranged the first ever syndicated loan with the Halifax. This was ground breaking as Halifax, the largest Building Society (Nationwide being second largest) were a massive competitor. A syndicated loan includes one or several partners to commit the funding on the same terms. I was proud to be involved at the centre of this.

As the market grew, the success stories of these housing transfers percolated and more funders became interested in the sector. My Nationwide team introduced Barclays then Abbey National and then Lloyds into the sector within our syndicates. This was great for the market as it generated more liquidity to fund the growing number and scale of the transfers.

For several years the transfers had a positive value attributed to them at an average of around £10,000 per dwelling. The council housing that was being transferred was generally terraced and/or semi detached houses, some low-rise flats and generally well spread across the catchment area of the Local Authority. However the model was then extended to more urban areas where the housing was less attractive. In these areas the catch up repairs were much more costly and more high-rise property was involved in heavy concentrations of property assets within inner cities. The impact of all these factors meant that there was rarely a capital sum payable to the council and often the properties were assessed as having a negative value and came with a dowry to get the catch up repairs initially funded. But this was where the funding and investment was really needed to improve housing standards in these more difficult areas and it had taken some considerable time before the funding community were confident enough in the transfer model to venture into this kind of project finance.

As you can imagine this rather complicated the funding process. However as Nationwide had developed a deep understanding of the sector, we remained committed, kept going and funded the largest urban housing stock transfers across the UK, starting with Tameside in 2000 with 19,000 dwellings, then Coventry Whitefriars also in 2000 with 20,500 dwellings. Next was Sunderland in 2001 with 36,000 dwellings and then Glasgow with more than 70,000 dwellings in 2003.

Back to the football

Through the process of leading all of this activity, I was introduced to many customers and professionals with sporting interests and it gave me a great opportunity to combine business and pleasure by attending some hand picked matches. By hand picked, I mean Stoke City matches and I had connected with a number of Stoke fans from all parts who I was now attending matches with as well as my usual team of mates.

The 1995/6 season showed continued progress under Lou Macari and after a slow start West Brom were their usual push over on 24th September, Pesch and Keen the scorers. We still had Keith Scott as a striking option, but oh my, he was not the future. Also John Gayle was in the squad. This was when Lou Macari did the best piece of football business I have ever witnessed. He swapped the ineffective Keith Scott for Mike Sheron from Norwich, yes the prolific Mike Sheron who went on a scoring spree later in the season breaking all sorts of records. Wow! Well done Lou and as for Norwich, well lads, you were well and truly stitched.

After winning soundly at Wolves 4 – 1 we had Chelsea to look forward to in the League Cup over two legs. We drew 0 – 0 at home in the first leg which meant we were really up against it away in the second leg. I hadn't been to Chelsea before and with Jeremy Allcock and Mike Taylor from work we drove down and found a pub to have a pre match beer. Ade was also joining us and was a bit late, but he was there in plenty of time to see the main action.

We were seated on what felt like temporary seating opposite the Shed end and the ground looked a bit of a mess. There was a healthy away following giving the locals some stick to our left. The Chelsea team sheet was impressive, Mark Hughes and Ruud Gullit in the team and Glenn Hoddle was Manager. They had just beaten Arsenal at the weekend with Hughes on the score sheet and there is a nice little spot in the programme where Steino says "Welcome to Stoke".

We stayed in the game well, there were few chances and at 0 – 0 half time, we were doing ok. We started brighter in the second half and after 70 minutes or so the ball was worked to Pesch who slipped past a defender and looked like he had all the goal to aim at, he picked his spot perfectly with a great shot from inside the box beating Kharine in the Chelsea goal easily and finding the top corner, cue delirious celebrations.

In an effort to get back into the game Chelsea brought Mark Stein on and while they created a few good chances, including one in particular falling to Steino, he proved that he is still a Stokie and fired wide. In the end a famous win, the only time I have ever seen my team win at Stamford Bridge.

On a recent pre-season trip to Hamburg we were talking about great players at the club and Steino came up, I felt he deserved a place in the discussion, but there was dispute about whether he really was that great given the league we were playing in etc. The answer is quite straightforward in my view, Steino played 63 times for Chelsea at the top level and scored 25 goals. For Stoke 139 times and netted 75 times. Sorry Owen, the stats do all the talking necessary, Steino is definitely one of our all time greats and I almost shed a tear to see him enter the pitch on Wilko's testimonial recently.

After the Chelsea game we stopped for a celebratory curry and drinks where Mike Taylor performed his usual party trick of asking for the hottest curry on the menu and then making the point to the waiters that he wanted it really hot, as if to goad them into loading it up with chilli. I have had several curries with him and despite what the cooks do to his food after he has encouraged them dangerously, he has always finished his meal and without, on the surface, any particular problem.

We got Newcastle at home in the next round and lightening didn't strike twice. We lost 4 – 0 at home and Ginola looked the part, even if he did spend half the time diving all over the pitch.

Back to the league, we were winning tight games by the odd goal and looking defensively pretty solid. The usual win 1 – 0 this time at West Brom included, Pesch scoring again in a poor game. Port Vale beat us 1 – 0, as they do, before Mike Sheron went on the record scoring spree, netting in seven consecutive games and Simon Sturridge was also partnering him now and looking sharp together.

Sheron scored one at Charlton in a 2 – 1 reverse, one at Derby which gave us the lead in a bad tempered affair at the Baseball ground, where there was some pretty nasty crowd trouble outside. Then he got a 90th minute winner at Luton which we never deserved, I remember walking back to the car and just laughing with Ade, as we had mugged an equalizer in the 88th minute and then Sheron bagged the winner totally against the run of play, home fans just couldn't believe it. He then got a 90th minute winner in the home game against Portsmouth, followed by a volley against Charlton to seal a 1 – 0 win. He didn't score at Sunderland in the next game, however he came back and scored at Millwall the following week where we won 3 – 2 after leading 3 – 0. There was a very large away following in the upper tier at the New Den creating a loud atmosphere. Sheron's final goal of the season was the winner at home to Southend on the final day and we were safely in the playoffs against Leicester City, who we had beaten home and away in the league.

The Play Off adventure just wasn't to be, we dominated away at Leicester in the first leg but drew 0 – 0 and at home it was full of tension and late in the game they scored from a Gary Parker left foot volley to which we could find no response. Leicester went on to win promotion to the Premier Division and we had to start all over again.

CHAPTER TEN
Our last season at the Vic

The 1996/7 season was our last at the Victoria Ground and it was to be an emotional farewell. Nationwide had become the new sponsors of the English Football League, which meant happy days in terms of some match day opportunities with mates and customers. First thing was first, I needed to find out who the coordinator of the tickets was at Nationwide for Stoke games and get on their good side. The Coordinator in this season was Jennifer Clarke and we hit it off straight away. She was attractive, a Stoke fan, the ticket coordinator and drank pints, it was like a dream come true.

We started the season ok with three wins and two draws, Mike Sheron scored in all five games! Then after two away defeats we took on Huddersfield at home and promptly went 2 – 0 down. A John Gayle goal just before half time set us up for the comeback and Mike Sheron scored twice late on to seal the win. First use of the sponsorship tickets came at West Brom where I took a customer who liked his football, though was a Villa fan. We won 2 – 0 in the usual expected fashion.

On 2nd October I attended the first game I had ever been to with my dad, we were staying at my brothers in Northolt and playing away at QPR and courtesy of Nationwide we had some good tickets. My dad was then seventy one and while we always chatted about the football and watched on TV together when we could, it was great to have him at a match with me and we were to go to a few others besides. Dad had lost the use of an eye through Glaucoma almost twenty years previously and was a bit unsteady on his feet, but I know he enjoyed the occasion.

Dad seemed to accept my obsession with Stoke City despite this being 100 miles from home, he always showed interest and I always felt that he wanted Stoke to do well for me. Even against his team Arsenal, he was always pleased for me when we got a good result. I asked him to a number of games and while he certainly wouldn't have managed the environment in the Boothen End, he did agree to come with me when I could get some seats and QPR was the first one of those. It took some persuading, and it was great.

My brother John also attended and my good friend Mark Webster, an Ipswich fan who I had been working with in the Housing team for quite a few years and who was to become my closest friend. After that Dad came with me to several games and I cherished this opportunity. Our record on his visits was pretty poor though and I wish I could take him to one of our matches in the Premier League. Sadly that's impossible now.

As for the QPR game, we took the lead through Graham Kavanagh from close range and it seemed to take him an age to convert as the ball fell to him just a few yards out. They equalized in the second half with a wonder goal from an overhead kick by Trevor Sinclair. A good game, and the occasion with my Dad and Brother there with me was what made it special.

My boss, Jeremy Wood who was Divisional Director of Commercial was a Wolves fan and we used the tickets to entertain at Molineaux in February, he won the spoils that day as Wolves won 2 – 0.

In the cups we struggled past Northampton, my hometown club. We had taken a large number of seats with work colleagues many eager to see a giant killing. But not this time and after a couple of beers beforehand, I was there to watch our vastly superior team wipe

89

the floor with the lowly cobblers. Well, having dispatched them 1 – 0 in the first leg (not terribly convincing) we then stumbled through this second leg without really threatening and then of course, it happened, they equalized with about ten minutes remaining. The horrible prospect of then being beaten was looming. We made it to extra time and began to shine with Mike Sheron eventually nabbing a brace to send us through. You can imagine my humble reaction to this, and quite close to ejection, I sat down again.

Arsenal were next. We took the lead at home through Sheron, but conceded late on and were heading to Highbury for the replay. My first visit to Arsenal saw a large and noisy away following. My brother who was now in a special department of the Metropolitan Police advised me to be careful as Stoke's Naughty contingent, usually *40*, were apparently going to be active. As it happens, the game was a good one, and the noisy away end got even noisier when Mike Sheron raced clear to score and to give us the lead. He raced to the right of the box and coolly slipped the ball past the keeper then the agonizing wait for the net to bulge began, it ended well. However just before the interval, the unpopular Ian Wright, who had a few minutes earlier chosen to blast the ball into the away fans end after he couldn't keep it in play, equalized. Arsenal over-powered us in the second half. We would however go on to have our moments against Arsenal and though they were my Dads club, I enjoyed watching us take them apart now and again and of course the special reaction that this always brought from Arsene Wenger.

And so to 5th May 1997, and the final game of the season and the last ever at the Vic. I was so desperate to maximize the experience at this final game that I used my season ticket to spend the first half on the Boothen End, for just one last time and then Jenny had also arranged for me to have tickets in the Directors Box. I know it's a bit greedy, but this meant so much to me and so arriving at the game on a bright and sunny day, my wife and I went into the lounge in the main stand. It was wonderful to watch all the preparations for the match.

At around 2.15pm all the old greats came out on to the pitch and made their way down toward the Boothen End. I walked down the stairs of the Main Stand and, with a thick Arran jumper covering my Stoke Top walked through the entrance to pitch side with my camera, and staying a safe distance from the entourage which included Sir Stan, Gordon Banks, Terry Conroy, Jimmy Greenhoff and John Ritchie I took a few photos of my own.

I know I shouldn't have been there but no one asked any questions as I walked up the touchline. When I got close to the Boothen End, I handed my camera to a bloke in the Boothen Paddock and asked him to take a shot of me in front of the Boothen End, my Boothen End. He obliged though gave me quite a strange look and I carried on following the real celebrities. Time was moving on so I wandered back from the entrance and back upstairs, left my jumper behind and made my way to the Boothen End in my usual spot with Ade and the gang. It was good, a feeling I still remember clearly.

As for the game, well it was against West Brom, so we obviously won, 2 − 1. Gerry McMahon got our first half goal which sent the Boothen End into raptures and that's how it was at half time, when I said goodbye to my mates and left the ground, re-entering in the main stand to watch the second half from that position and take several more photos. Graham Kavanagh scored our second and despite a goal back for West Brom we were destined to win this match. I stayed in the ground for ages afterwards, watching the crowd, looking at the empty stadium and knowing that I would never see it again. In the distance through the gap between the Boothen End and the Butler Street Stand, you could see the new ground almost complete. That shiny new stadium would be our home next

season. All this meant the end for Uncle Tom's Cabin as without the
football business, it had no hope of surviving.

CHAPTER ELEVEN
The Brit 1997/98

The following season was always going to be different. There was a level of excitement as the group of lads I had been going to matches for ages orchestrated the choice of seats at the new Britannia Stadium. They had picked out some brilliant seats right behind the goal in the Boothen End in Block 21, Rows 18 and 19. My seat is 320 and it remains my second home. We still argue about whose seat is absolutely dead centre behind the goal and I know that I am right to believe it's mine. We were used to turning up from the pub seconds before kick off and then muscling our way to the usual spot and even if that was congested, the first corner of the game always presented the opportunity to restore the equilibrium in our patch at the back of the Boothen End. Now, we had to find a new pre match bar, sort out the parking and get to the match and to our specified seats.

Steve, one of the team, sussed out a place to get a pre match beer just over the bridge at Heron Cross in a broken down bar that we called Beirut, for obvious reasons. We knew this place was going to be condemned at any time and Steve was again on the case recommending Fenton Bowling Club which was in much better condition and had loads of outside space as well as a large interior and good parking.

It has been our home now for 20 years and counting, its handy, friendly and we all stand under one of the roofed shelters furthest away from the bar entrance which we have occupied at every home match until the present day. The staff are excellent, the Wrights pies are great and dead cheap and there is always a couple of good real ales on offer.

For the official opening game of the season, I was not with the lads, I was in the Director's Box with a mate from work, Mike Taylor (that's Mike the very hot curry guy). We were late for the match and managed to persuade the parking attendant that we had a car park space allocated, which in the confusion and mayhem around the ground, he let us through. So we managed to get through reception and up to Level Three. It wasn't my first actual match at the ground, as we played Rochdale in the first round of the League Cup and escaped with a draw after a 90th minute thunderbolt by Graham Kavanagh, not a great game but a great way to finish.

In this first league game and the official opener at the Britannia, I was seated a few rows behind Willie Carson who was associated with our opponents Swindon Town. We expected to win and when Richard Forsyth scored in the first half, surely there could only be one result on a historic day for our club in its new home. Not quite, Swindon not only equalized but went on to get the winner fairly late on, not the start we had all anticipated.

Afterwards we were in the Gordon Banks Suite having a drink and Mike and I had spotted Sir Stanley Matthews going into the Chairman's Suite on the same level. He took my souvenir programme from me and marched into their lounge, returning moments later with Sir Stan's signature on it. The programme resides with my collection including the souvenir programme from the final game at the Victoria Ground, which also bears Sir Stan's autograph.

The facilities were impressive, the view incredible and I was particularly struck by how the stadium looked once all of the crowd had disappeared, it was amazing and I knew then that it would become a special home for us, though not before some teething problems. The teething problems included a decade of near hell, occasionally punctuated with an outstanding game or two. Eventually though, we did click into gear and were able to embrace the power of our unique stadium.

Lou Macari had departed the club and Chic Bates was in charge. I am still not quite sure why Lou wasn't still in charge but it was clear that there was an under current of unrest at the club which manifested itself negatively. Results deteriorated after a useful start where we had won away at both Middlesborough (at their new Riverside stadium, a near replica of the Britannia, but with the corners filled in) and Manchester City. Before the wheels fell off, we beat Wolves 3 – 0 at home where I entertained some Wolves fans who were good customers of Nationwide and while I was thrilled by the score line, it did not tell the story of the match where we were outplayed. One high spot was the form of Peter Thorne, signed from Swindon for half a million, a true striker who was a big lad, a great header of the ball and fearless.

Away at West Brom we kept our remarkable run against them going and drew 1 – 1 with Thorney again on the score sheet, but I was absent from the home game against Birmingham on 10th January 1998 as my oldest son, Daniel was born two days earlier.

I worked with a good friend and colleague, Jeremy Allcock, a Birmingham fan and who had attended the game at St Andrews with me when all the trouble broke out a few years earlier. He had bought my new son, Daniel, a baby Blues top. When we played them just two after his birth, they won 7 – 0. The scenes at that match and after the next game at home to Bradford City (which we managed to win 2 – 1, with Thorney again on target) prompted Peter Coates to resign as Chairman. It was all going wrong.

I visited Crewe on 13th April where we lost 2 – 0 in a game we actually played quite well in and after a vital home win against Norwich we had just two games to save our season and place in Division One. The first was away at Sunderland. I was at the stadium of light among a 41,214 crowd, and took the opportunity to take some customers to this most impressive stadium. This was where I first experienced the sounds of Prokoviev vibrating through the stadium and Sunderland, who finished third and eventually lost the amazing play off final against Charlton, easily overcame us 3 – 0. We had just one more chance and even a win might not be enough to save us now. Our opponents were Manchester City, themselves in peril a point worse off than us.

It was very nervy at this final game, and I attended with my Dad again, my Uncle Dave and a contact from Abbey National, Richard Hughes who was a Man City fan. I enjoyed the time with my dad before the match, at the game and afterwards as we stayed behind to let the crowds subside, but was distraught by our relegation in our first year at our new stadium. By the time Peter Thorne scored the first of his two goals, we were 3 – 0 down and heading for a 5 – 2 home defeat and relegation (together with Man City for whom the win couldn't save them either).

Earlier in the season, after Chic Bates had departed, Chris Kamara arrived and was a popular figure with the fans from his short spell as a player at the club. However we proceeded to lose eight from eight (including the home game against Birmingham) before he resigned and Alan Durban took the reigns for the final set of games.

The 1998/9 season began again in the third tier of English football with a new manager at the helm, Brian Little, the silky skillful ex midfielder who seemed very articulate. We had the best and newest stadium in the league and started like a train. On a hot day in August we won comfortably 3 – 1 at my home town club Northampton. A

96

good performance was greeted by a large away following where both Peter Thorne and Dean Crowe were on target and it was all started off by Kavanagh with a well taken penalty after 7 minutes. We won at home versus Macclesfield and then I was off to Preston for my first visit with some customers from New Progress Housing Association, who were locals from Leyland. The Nationwide sponsorship tickets got us some great seats in the main stand and access to the lounge and by half time, I needed a drink as we were 2 – 0 behind. We responded through Dean Crowe, then went 3 – 1 behind and in an amazing game equalized with two goals from Graham Kavanagh, the second a penalty. Then, in the 85th minute, Crowe was sent through and we had a chance to win it, he coolly slotted in and we went wild at the back of the stand.

Next up was a regulation win at home to Oldham, where Kyle Lightbourne scored for us in a 2 - 0 win. I was in two minds about the Lightbourne signing, he cost half a million which I begrudged paying to Coventry City and he wasn't great. But he was a trier and as one of the only Bermudian players in the football league was at least busting a gut for the club.

Next up Colchester away and Ade and I were on our way to Layer Road where we had Nationwide tickets again as the away section was sold out. Not a great game but after a long slow drive, it was lit up by a strike from outside the penalty box from Kavanagh which secured our fifth win in a row.

One more home win against Bournemouth meant six in a row before we faced Fulham away in midweek. Fulham, with Chris Coleman in their defence, were promotion favourites despite our roaring start to the season and this game promised much. We lost 1 – 0 in a tight game before a large crowd of 12,055 at Craven Cottage.

We kept it all going with a last minute Lightbourne goal from a glancing header against Millwall and we were still believing that we could achieve a rapid promotion. Ade and I had arranged to travel to Sincil Bank, Lincoln on 17th October but Ade's wife Dawn was unwell so I trekked up on my own and was glad I did as we came back from 1 – 0 down to win with two good headers and it was good to stand on an old fashioned terrace once again and celebrate in the usual way.

Our side now included Larus Sigurdsson, a talented footballing centre half and also David Oldfield who was still proving his worth at this level and I was travelling to more and more games with Garry Nash, a local Stoke City fan in Northampton who had stopped going a number of years earlier and we struck up a good friendship and took the opportunity to travel anywhere we could.

As our season petered out after such a great start, it all seemed such a waste and Brian Little was showing distinct signs of stress. The away game at Millwall wasn't a game I could get to though I was following the updates closely. We were soon 1 – 0 down, then they had a man sent off. Then we went 2 – 0 down before they had a second man sent off, so at half time we were two goals behind and with a whole half to play against nine men. Yep, you guessed it final score 3 – 0 to Millwall, god knows what the band of Stoke fans who had made that trip thought! Brian Little left in the close season but not before I somehow felt the inclination to drive all the way to Gillingham and watch us get thumped 4 – 0, we were woeful. Gillingham ended up in the playoffs and reached the final in that amazing final against Man City where they were leading 2 – 0 with three minutes to go and ended up conceding two late goals and then being defeated in extra time as Man City began their march back to the big time.

Gillingham's manager was none other than Tony Pulis.

By this time I had completed some additional banking exams (the Financial Studies Diploma) that not many people did. Having got through the 8 original subjects of the Associate of Chartered Institute of Bankers qualification (ACIB), I think I must have caught the study and exam bug later in life because at school, college and during the first few years at work I struggled to be any better than pretty average, just about surmounting the pass mark threshold on a number of occasions.

Having developed the inclination to study, I continued this by embarking on an MBA on a part time, distance learning basis at Sheffield Hallam University. Nationwide generously sponsored me to do this.

I was doing pretty well at Nationwide and during my time as Head of Housing, where we arranged and lent large sums to Housing Associations, we secured a pre-eminent position in the market. I had assembled a strong team of funding experts and an opportunity arose for me to assume new and wider responsibilities. Graham Beale, the then Divisional Director of Commercial and soon to be FD and then CEO of the Society, invited me to Head up the Property Finance team and its 160 colleagues located throughout offices in the UK. This was a great opportunity for me to advance as a senior leader in the business. It also gave rise to even more opportunity to combine office and customer visits with trips to Stoke away games across a larger geography!

Summer had arrived and for Stoke, time to go again. Our Superman powers had instilled us with much optimism, probably more than was proportionate. We had a new manager, Gary Megson, not a universally popular choice, but a hard working and honest man and one who grew on the fans as we started to cement a strong position in the league and began to deliver several consistent performances.

I saw a couple of very good away wins from the comfort of the Directors Box with customers and Ade, starting at Cambridge where we won 3 – 1 in the sunshine and then midweek at Cardiff in a 2 – 1 win there Thorney and James O'connor steered us through. It was quite tasty getting away from the ground afterwards but we were fine with that after an accomplished performance and three points in the bag. Unfortunately, Gary Megson had to make way for the new owners choice of manager, Gudjon Thordarson who was pretty experienced and had managed the national team in Iceland. He soon recruited various Icelandic players, including his son Bjarni.

My favourite game of the season was away at Wycombe. I not only got to visit Adams Park for the first time but then, after entertaining customers, a couple of mates and my brother to drinks and dinner before the game, saw my team cruise to a 4 – 0 victory. I had a bet on a 2 – 0 win with Kavanagh to score the first goal and at 80 – 1 this looked good at half time as the score was 2 – 0 and Kav had netted first. The rest of my group were keen for the game to finish at this score line, but I was delighted to see the additional two goals to finish the rout. We stopped for a couple of beers on the way home and other than for the clutch going in my Company car on the way home, being gratefully driven by a colleague, Richard Furniss, a passionate Newcastle fan, we would have been safely in our beds at midnight instead of the actual 2.30am it ended up being. No matter it was memorable as the tow truck brought us home.

It was an entertaining season and as we headed for Brentford away in that narrow lower tier of terracing behind the goal. It was brilliant to see Peter Thorne sliding in fearlessly to net our winner in the 60th minute. Thorney showed his bravery time and again during this season in which he scored 30 goals, a rare landmark for a striker at Stoke City.

Away at Wigan on 26th February 2000, just days after the anniversary of Sir Stanley Matthews death there was a large Stoke following at The JJB. We took he lead through a well taken goal through Kav and though they equalized, James O'Connor scored from a well placed header to give us the win. Wigan is quite a strange club, there is only a modest level of intrinsic local home support (it's a Rugby League town) and other than the backing of Dave Whelan, they would never have figured as a Premier League team and winners of the FA Cup (in their relegation year). At the match, there was some unrest in the stands to our right and then afterwards between Stoke fans and the Police, but nothing worthy of the headlines on Radio 5 Live which I felt compelled to phone in and put the record straight on the drive home. Anyway, another away win and we were heading in the right direction.

We were heading for the playoffs with Preston and Burnley in the automatic promotion places. Even our six match winning streak at the end of the season where Thorney scored in five successive games, couldn't clinch us automatic promotion.

I attended many away games during the season including one other using the Nationwide tickets, this time at Scunthorpe where Ade and I saw Stoke win 2 – 0 in a very accomplished performance with Thorney scoring both. Then, away at Reading on the last day of the season where a massive away following saw us fall to a 1 – 0 defeat, but it didn't dull the success we had achieved. To calm Stoke fans at the end, they even announced that we were safely in the play offs (despite the score line) and we left relatively happy.

In other competitions were we crap, except for the League Trophy, the equivalent of the Autoglass Trophy, where we reached

101

the final once again, paved with a 3 – 1 win at Rochdale in the first leg of the semi final which I managed to attend on my way driving to Dundee. A long drive, but worth every minute. Our opponents in the final were Bristol City and this time the Old Wembley was a sell out. A great day out at Wembley followed and it was great for my brother to again be with me on the big occasion. We took the lead through Kav in the first half and while they equalized in the second half, Thorney was on hand to slide in a brave winner in the 82nd minute, so we were able to celebrate once again.

CHAPTER TWELVE
Play Off Hell

Back to the league, we had Gillingham in the playoffs and we were playing well. In our home game, the first leg we were great, we raced into a two goal lead and then from a horrible scramble they somehow got one back before half time. Thorney scored a third to put us completely in control at 3 – 1. As we neared the end of the game with the relative comfort of a two goal lead, the very annoying Andy Hessentaller picked up the ball and from thirty yards shot hopefully. It sailed into the top corner and the (very small) number of visiting Gillingham fans celebrated as though they had won.

So we trekked down to Gillingham for the second leg in midweek, it's a long way as I have said before, I was travelling with Ade and Garry and met my mate Mike Roche (Mike the Mack he was affectionately called due to his long Chicago gangster coat). We had a beer in a local pub where I had to bribe the barman to serve us as it was so busy and we took our double round outside. In a small group of mainly Gillingham fans, we were all looking forward to heading for Wembley, not for a minor cup competition, but a play off final. A small loud and arrogant guy turned up pretty soon after sporting a shiny, cheap looking suit and dark rimmed glasses. He smiled at his Gillingham fan mates and said, "Thorne is out; Asaba is in". The Gillingham fans seemed happy to accept that this information was indeed correct, and while for us Thorne being out would be a huge blow, we didn't know at that point that this news was accurate. The messenger at the pub was Paul Scally, Gillingham Chairman and owner and he was right, our main striker was out and their main striker, Carl Asaba, was in. I hate Paul Scally.

As for the game, we were on an open terrace, the view was pretty poor and we were well fenced in. It was a very brave Stoke performance. You know I am sick and tired of recounting our "brave" performances, what I wanted was for us to win at any cost, sod the bravery. In this instance we had two players sent off, Graham Kavanagh and Clive Clarke for relatively minor offenses by Rob Styles and we were incensed. We held out to half time at 0 – 0 and though they scored in the 55th minute, we held out at 1 – 0 for extra time. Unfortunately toward the end of the first period of extra time they scored again through Iffy Onuora and now we needed to score with nine men to stay in the tie. Toward the very end it nearly happened as Paul Connor hit a snap shot from inside the box at our end and the ball agonizingly struck the post and rebounded away. They immediately went down the other end and scored again which finished the match. This was one of the worst feelings I have had at a football match.

They went on to beat Wigan in the play off final at Wembley and were promoted to the second tier of the league and we were left in the old Division three (now called Division One as the old Division One was now the Premier League and the old Division Two was called the Championship), so Division One really meant the old Division three, the third tier of English football and you know, they could change the name to whatever they want, it wouldn't make us feel any better.

Before the start of the 2000/01 season on 29th July my second son was born, Thomas. Soon to be affectionately known as Tonka. It would be a few years before I would take him to a match, and in the meantime, we had work to do to escape this godforsaken division.

We had some real hope at the start of the following season with an influx of overseas players, mostly Icelandic including the impressive Brynjar Gunnarsson, who acclimatized to the football league better than most and possessed real class. Wayne Thomas also joined and was to become a fans favourite and in addition, we were waiting for Rikki Dadason to join us from his Icelandic team and he was said to be the striker who would propel us up the league and to promotion.

It ended up being a bit of a weird season. We were knocked out of the FA Cup by the mighty non league Nuneaton Borough as I have covered earlier. In the league cup it was all going so well, we won convincingly at York City which gave me the chance to cross off another long distance ground from my list. I stood on the open terrace at York's Bootham Crescent and watched a performance of great accomplishment, it's not often you get to see Stoke scoring five away from home (or even at home for that matter). Then we knocked out Premier League Charlton Athletic, after taking a 2 – 1 lead to the Valley and then in a brilliant game that Mike the Mack and I attended, we held them to a 3 – 2 score line in normal time and then, having had a player sent off, proceeded to equalize through one of the best goals I have ever seen.

Stefan Thordarson a talented Icelandic player collected the ball in our half and raced toward the corner of their box, where he unleashed a thunderbolt into the top corner. We went bananas and while they regained the lead to make it 4 – 3 we held on to that and won on away goals after extra time had finished. A fabulous game and one where our bravery led to the victory we deserved, rather than us narrowly missing out.

Our reward for those heroics was a home tie on 1st November against Barnsley and Rikki Dadason's first start for the Potters. He came on with a few minutes to go with the score line 2 – 2 against the Championship team and made an immediate impact heading home from a corner to seal the win. We were all convinced this was

105

it, the missing link to the puzzle and another striker capable of 20 goals plus per season.

Liverpool, were our next opponents in the fourth round and if ever we needed bringing down to earth, wow. Strange though, a massive crowd of over 27,000 had packed the Britannia and expectation was high. In the first couple of minutes their keeper Arphexad was hesitant to make a clearance and Thorne robbed him of the ball close to goal. Both keeper and Thorne were on the deck and Thorne responded the quicker and reached the ball first and from a forty five degree angle and six yards out with no keeper to beat he merely had to roll it in. He shot firmly but inexplicably struck the ball against the post rather than into the empty net. Our chance had gone and what an amazing chance it was. Before we knew what was going on they were ahead and then 2 – 0 and it didn't stop. A record 8 – 0 defeat including a Robbie Fowler hat trick.

Of course we enjoyed getting our own back more recently when we hammered them 6 – 1 on Steven Gerrard's final game for the club, more about that one later.

Our other cup run was in the equivalent of the Autoglass Trophy which we had won twice. I didn't see the first game against Scarborough but travelled in very wintery conditions to Halifax in January with Garry from Northampton to tick this new ground off my list, the Shay stadium.

Halifax Town AFC had regained league status in 1998 and were enjoying their time away from non league football and as I have mentioned previously, Halifax was a huge competitor of Nationwide. One of my ex bosses at Nationwide, Mike Lazenby a likeable if sometimes controversial character, who first welcomed me into the Housing Association senior team was now Divisional Director of Marketing. When an opportunity to sponsor Halifax Town arose and the Halifax Building Society hesitated, he seized the moment and sealed a deal right under their noses. He made it even worse for them by agreeing to paint a massive *Nationwide* logo on the roof of the main stand easily visible across the town and especially by the rival building society's Head Office, you had to laugh.

Garry and I had left Northampton after work and were on a tight timescale. Just a mile or so from home on the M1 the traffic stopped. We spoke to one another saying that at least there weren't emergency vehicles visible so hopefully it would be a short volume of traffic type delay. Within a minute two police cars and an ambulance flew past on the hard shoulder and we new things were worse than we had feared. Luckily when we reached the point of the incident the bump that had occurred wasn't too bad and when we got going again we made up some ground. The next issue was the weather, it wasn't quite snowing but was freezing and our next fear as we passed Sheffield and toward North Yorkshire was that the game would be postponed.

On arriving in Halifax, we dumped the car by a pub and even had time for a quick pint where we bumped into Owen and quickly drained our beer to get to the match. There was a healthy number of Stoke fans in the ground within a crowd of 1,917. We started slowly and soon conceded, this became worse only a few moments later. We had travelled 160 miles in freezing weather only to be 2 – 0 down to Halifax Town. Great. I decided enough was enough and went to get the pies for Garry and I and also Ade who had travelled across from Warrington.

Not surprisingly the pie queue was quite long after that second goal went in and half way through the queuing a loud cheer went up from the away fans, we had scored, Dadason with the goal I never saw. By this time I was at the front of the queue and had hold of the three hot pies. Just as I was paying we scored again and while I was glad that my team had scored, I was pretty pissed off that I had missed both goals. The lads enjoyed their pies and were of course in tears of laughter as I returned.

It was 2 – 2 at half time and we now hoped for a second half onslaught and please, no extra time! By now it was freezing fog and not much of the pitch was visible. In the 90th minute we scored the winner, up at the other end of the ground and I couldn't see that one either from the away terrace. So I had not seen any of our three goals and now faced the long trip home. In the semi final of the competition which followed after we beat Walsall 4 – 0 in the quarter final, our recent nemesis returned in the form of Port Vale who defeated us 2 – 1 after extra time so we were denied a return to Wembley.

In the league, home crowds were around 13,000 which was reasonable but still meant the ground was barely half full on most occasions, a real shame to see and we just had to do something about it. At the end of August we played away at Reading and I had invited some more Stokie contacts to the game with dinner beforehand. My brother also joined us and we were hoping for a great night out. The Madejski stadium is well put together and the facilities are very good indeed. I was joined by Eric Cooper and Allan Smith two great guys, both complete Stokies, who I had met through work connections and it appeared they were a good omen. We established a 3 – 1 lead and with just a few minutes remaining we were surely going to secure the win. Eventual score 3 – 3, and while we shipped two late goals, this was still a good performance and one that gave us hope.

My second trip to Swansea at the Vetch Field was far less eventful than my first, though the result wasn't as positive. We were fifteen minutes late arriving by which time we were 2 – 0 down. A late consolation by Kyle Lightbourne wasn't enough and we were struggling again for consistency.

108

My next away trip was to Wrexham a relative local derby and lots of Stoke fans selling out the allocation. I managed to get hold of the Nationwide tickets again and took Garry and his son Jamie who was ten at the time. The visit to the Racecourse Ground meant another new ground for me and two goals in the first half eased the nerves. The first was a debatable penalty which was coolly slotted home by Thordarson. We went on to win 2 – 1 and were back on track. Northampton away was next and again a large contingent joining me from work in an entertaining game in midweek where we couldn't hold on to the lead twice and ended up 2 – 2. This wasn't actually a bad result in the end as Wayne Thomas was dismissed at the start of the second half.

It wasn't long before we were playing the Cobblers again this time at Stoke and I had high hopes of a resounding win. We took the lead when Andy Cooke scored well from a Peter Thorne knockdown. Then inexplicably conceded from a soft effort that our Icelandic keeper, Birkir Kristinsson (who had played 74 times for his country) seemed to smother but let the ball squirm under his body and through his legs for a bizarre equalizer.

As the season drew to a close we were again in play off territory and we resoundingly beat Swindon on the final game of the league season to finish in 5th place with 77 points. But on this day, 5th May, I was as interested in Coventry's relegation match as in Stoke's play off push.

We drew Walsall in the play offs, they were a solid side who had finished above us in the league and had beaten us at their Bescot Stadium and had drawn against us at the Britannia, this was always going to be tight. A big crowd saw us draw the first leg at home 0 – 0, though to be fair, they were the better side and could well have won that game. Don Goodman was now playing for them and just as well he had an off day. For the away leg the tickets sold out quickly being such a close and convenient local derby and so I invited a number of handpicked guests and booked a table for pre match dinner at Walsall with seats right over by the away fans. There were a great many Stoke fans who had exactly the same idea. The usual culprits were there, Owen, Eric, Allan, Garry and Jamie and also a colleague from work who followed me from Barclays to Nationwide, Ian Greatrex, who was a local from the Walsall area.

When the team sheet was handed out before kick off we were all eagerly looking to see who was selected. To our complete astonishment, Peter Thorne, our leading goal scorer who had notched 19 goals, was on the bench. We were flabbergasted and another example of the kind of strange decision making we had become accustomed to from Gudjon Thordarson, who hadn't picked a striker in a game we had to win.

Despite this we took a first half lead through a wonderful strike by Graham Kavanagh. He struck from twenty five yards with a thunderbolt and we celebrated wildly. We were good value and for once it looked like the rather odd game plan was going to work. Then, on the stroke of half time from a Walsall corner, Gavin Ward our keeper, a big strong lad who had done well for us, let the ball slip through his hands under little pressure and they had equalized through an own goal. We were completely stunned. After the restart, Walsall never looked back and scored three times in fifteen minutes to end the tie. Only then did Gudjon throw Peter Thorne on. He scored almost immediately but it was too little too late and again our play off hopes were dashed.

CHAPTER THIRTEEN
More Icelandic Tales &
Millennium Stadium

Pressure had been building on Gudjon to get Stoke out of this league. But other clubs appeared to have even more appetite to leave the division behind, especially Cardiff City who had money to burn. They first bought Graham Kavanagh from us for £1 million and then the dagger to the heart, Peter Thorne sold to the same competitor club in the league for an even greater sum.

Kav got some pretty rough treatment when he returned to play at the Brit and it definitely seemed to affect his performance. While I was unhappy about his departure, I think we saw the best of him and the contract he accepted at Cardiff was obviously attractive for him. We in return received a fair transfer fee, so I wasn't as angry about this as many other Stoke fans. Similarly with Peter Thorne, he had done a great strikers job for us, and came back to haunt us by scoring a hat trick for Cardiff at the Brit, which to his credit he celebrated very humbly.

The outgoings gave us the chance to bring in some new faces and lets face it, the guys hadn't made the difference in getting us promoted in the last two years so maybe it was time for a change. Peter Handyside joined as a solid centre half and captain and then one of my favourite players to ever join the club, the Belarus player, Sergei Shtanyuk, who epitomized how a battling centre half should play. He was hard as nails and as I have said before, we love our centre halves at Stoke. He was the best defensive header of a ball in the division and took absolutely no prisoners.

We had certainly steadied the ship at the back and just needed goals to deliver the points required to stay near the top of the division. We had also enlisted the Dutchman Peter Hoekstra who had represented Holland five times including at the 1996 Euros. He was injury prone, but pure class on the ball. Some might say a luxury, others would say sheer brilliance.

I had been in Manchester on 23rd October with my North West team and we were playing Chesterfield away so it was a great opportunity to nip across the Peak District National Park and watch the team. What a dramatic winding journey, it took longer than I anticipated but worth every minute, not a trip I would want to take on in the middle of Winter though. Another new ground for me at Saltergate and a busy away following on the open terrace. We conceded from a strong header and had to fight our way back. The comeback came with two goals from the maestro Hoekstra. First a snap shot which crept in at the near post, and which their keeper should have done better. Then a penalty in the final minute right in front of the baying Stoke fans. Hoekstra made no mistake and enjoyed the celebrations.

Two weeks later it was Swindon away and with a handful of Nationwide tickets, I travelled with Garry, Jamie and my eldest son Daniel for his very first game. We met Eric there too and enjoyed a celebratory drink after a resounding victory, with the only downside being that I had a bet on at 4 – 0 and we ended up winning 3 – 0 with James O'Connor going close late on.

The crowds were growing again now as the expectation began to take hold especially after we beat Brentford, who were challenging for automatic promotion, 3 – 2 at home on 10th November. In between the two games we were away at Wigan and I was keen to go. This time I took a local mate, John Smith and Garry and we arrived in good time to enjoy a couple of local pies at the ground. We went 1 – 0 down early on and then equalized quickly afterwards through Vandeurzen, but after that we were terrible and lost 6 – 1 and it felt like a very long way home. Neil Cutler was in goal and had a stinker, which was a shame as many thousands of Stoke fans had travelled to fill the away side of the ground.

We finished the season on 80 points and again found ourselves in 5th place and in the playoffs once again where we received the hardest play off draw available against Cardiff. They had taken two of our top players and had finished one place and three points above us.

We were at home in the first leg again and this time were dominated by a strong Cardiff side in front of a 21,000 crowd including a loud contingent from South Wales. Cardiff had a wealth of attacking options including our own Peter Thorne, Rob Earnshaw and man mountain, Leo Fortune West. Earnshaw used his pace to give the visitors the lead in the first half and doubled their lead in the second half scoring from a rebound off the post. There were some nasty scenes in the crowd at this point and the game was held up for five minutes as the Stoke faithful felt pangs of déjà vu in the playoffs once again. Late on we grabbed a lifeline through a Deon Burton half volley at the Boothen End, very well struck, and that's how the first leg finished.

Now for the real hard work, away at Cardiff in the second leg where there was massive expectation. The final would be played at the Millennium Stadium also in Cardiff and it seemed inevitable that they would seal their fate in the final played in their home town. There was also the small matter of the crowd trouble at Stoke which led to away fans only allowed to visit if coached in from Stoke – not very convenient for me living in Northampton.

I couldn't make the second leg at Cardiff due to work commitments, however I managed to get to Stoke just in time to watch a live screening of the match on a huge screen erected in front of the main stand where many thousands of Stoke fans chose to watch the match.

This was a really tough ask. They had wheeled dignitaries to the match at Ninian Park including Neil Kinnock, all brought there to watch their inevitable progress to the final and then surely there could be no stopping them at the Millennium stadium. We had to win, no other result would do and we began playing pretty well without creating many chances. The relative small band of travelling supporters were making themselves heard in the 19,000 crowd where there was a sense of some nervousness. A good thing. Half time came and it was 0 – 0.

We continued to press without really creating an opening and time began to drift away. You could sense the home crowd just wanted the match to be over. We were in the last minute now and another brave but not quite good enough performance and result seemed on the cards. Clive Clarke had advanced down the wing and reached the byline before cutting the ball back where James O'Connor was waiting about ten yards out. He steered the ball goal wards, but without great power and it bobbled toward the far corner. It all felt like slow motion and it was clear the keeper wasn't going to get there, but there were several other players crowding the box. One of those was Graham Kavanagh and as he tried to clear, the ball went through his legs and amazingly ended just inside the far post and in the net. We had won the game and were sending the tie into Extra Time.

I don't know what it must have been like in the ground itself, but I do know that the mental that ensued in the main stand and that spilled out onto the pitch including the dancing stewards, was a sight

114

to behold. It calmed down and we now had it all to play for. Thirty minutes left. Now the nerves were really beginning to jangle. The first period was pretty equal and no further score or clear chances created. In the second period we won a free kick just outside the box. It surprised us that James O'Connor looked like he was going to take the kick, and he sent a waist high ball toward goal and into the wall. In the wall was one of our lads, Soulemane Oulare who tried to get out of the way. The ball hit him on the backside and with the keeper wrong footed it entered the net in the other corner. Cue another even more frantic celebration. They had a chance or two after that but in the end we had gone there and against all the odds had defeated them 2 – 0. It was us, not Cardiff City who would be playing in the Play off final at the Millennium Stadium and this time, we really had to make the most of it.

That evening remains one of the most memorable in all my years supporting Stoke City. From our eventual promotion that year, it was a real turning point, without which we may well be nowhere near the dizzy heights that we enjoy today.

And so to the playoff final, to be played at the magnificent Millennium Stadium where all of the big finals were taking place while Wembley was deconstructed and New Wembley created. The Millennium was for me the ideal sporting venue, now since January 2016 named the Principality Stadium, sponsored by the Welsh Building Society, the Principality. Firstly its big with a capacity of 74,500 and was primarily constructed for the 1999 Rugby World Cup for which Wales were the main host with seven of the forty one matches being played there including the final. It has a rarely used retractable roof, quite a handy feature in South Wales. Unlike many large National Stadia, such as old Wembley, fans are much closer to the pitch housed in steep stands which deliver an excellent view all around.

When constructing the bars around the stadium, "joy machines" were installed which can pour twelve pints in less than twenty seconds, these should be mandatory at every Premier League football ground! An example of their value is that during a Wales versus France rugby match, 63,000 fans drank 77,184 pints of beer. Not a massive number you might say, but consider this, it was almost double the 44,000 pints consumed by a similar number of fans at the game at Twickenham, where the Guinness takes forever! Also, the Millennium benefits from its position in the centre of Cardiff which is always buzzing with bars and restaurants before kick off and is a short five or ten minute stroll. Quite different from Wembley which is sat in the middle of almost nowhere and in a set of surroundings that are dilapidated and unimpressive.

Another feature of the Millennium Stadium is that the construction cost was around £150 million, in other words you could get six of these for the one new Wembley. A great value, well located and brilliant stadium.

It suffered from a so called "away team hoodoo" as all of the first eleven major cup finals hosted there were won by the teams occupying the home dressing room. Guess which dressing room we would be occupying, yes, the away team dressing room.

As sponsor of the English Football League, the play off finals were naturally a big deal for Nationwide and they always tried to make the most of these showcase events by putting on a good show. I had bagged a table for ten in the Millennium Lounge and intended to squeeze every ounce out of this rare opportunity.

We had left home fairly early on a lovely warm Spring day and headed to meet the lads at Strensham Services at the junction of the M5 and M50. From there the journey into Cardiff is very scenic, avoiding the M4 and the Severn Bridge crossing. I travelled with

Garry, his wife Lynn and son Jamie and we were all in great spirits on a glorious sunny morning.

I remember leaving the house as (my now ex-wife) said to me, "don't you come back here and tell me this was the best day of your life". So I didn't tell her that on my return, even though it almost was (with the exception of the birth of my children).

We arrived at the ground even before the hospitality areas had opened and were lucky enough to have a car park space underneath the stadium. We dumped the car and walked around the impressive arena, which looked fabulous in the sunshine. The rest of the lads had travelled to park by a bar set up fairly locally and were in situ at the bar before we had gained entry to the stadium. At the gates we immediately met Eric who gave us all a hug, he was a bit beside himself with excitement and then as they opened the hospitality doors, the quite large crowd that had built up entered the ground. We made our way to the well appointed lounge and started with a beer, found our table and then went for a look at the ground from the inside where the Stoke players were also surveying the scene. We waved and gratefully received responses from the lads and felt good about the occasion. Owen, also from Nationwide and still in charge of the Stoke City ticket allocations having assumed this responsibility from the generous Jennifer, wasn't with us on this occasion. Instead he was sat in the Royal Box just a few rows back and lording it with the good and the great, including my bosses boss, Stuart Bernau who was an Executive Director at Nationwide and a good guy to boot. Stuart was instrumental in bringing me to Nationwide from Barclays all those years earlier.

Back in the lounge the drinks were flowing and the food was excellent. Though I wasn't especially hungry, I could still drink and so took advantage and half an hour from kick off was really quite ready for the match. Before we took our excellent seats with a perfect view bang on the half way line, Eric got everyone to hold hands around the table and said a few words. It was like a prayer and we were all quite happy to accept any divine intervention going. Mike the Mack was also with us reflecting on that horrible play off experience we had endured at Gillingham.

Inside the ground the tens of thousands of Stoke fans were filling up the three tiers to our left and spreading a long way around the stadium on both our side and in the opposite stand. Our opponents, Brentford, managed by the experienced Steve Coppell, were not so well supported and barely filled half an end, surely this had to be our day?

It was all a bit emotional as kick off approached, singing the national anthem in Cardiff and as the game got underway. It was a cagey start though we were fairly comfortable. As the half wore on we looked the more likely. From an Arnar Gunnlaugsson corner which big Chris Iwelomo managed to flick on, Deon Burton on loan (and who had given us a chance in the semi finals with the late goal at home to Cardiff when we were 2 – 0 down), scored a poachers goal from close range. The relief was there for all to see in the crowd and I gave everyone of my table guests a big hug as we celebrated this vital foothold in the game.

We continued to look the stronger and defensively with Handyside and Sergei were very solid at the back. Just before half time we won a free kick just outside the box. Bjarni, the managers son was over the ball and sent a low free kick toward goal which struck Burgess and sent the keeper the wrong way, we were 2 – 0 up and it felt like heaven.

Half time arrived and chance for some refreshment that never tasted so good. We were in complete control and it was totally ours to lose now.

118

I don't remember much about the second half. Brentford were a bit better but couldn't penetrate and we looked likely to add to our tally late on, but didn't manage to do this. I just wanted the game to end and for us to accept the trophy and win our promotion. This of course happened and with it we broke the away team dressing room Hoodoo. I remember the Nationwide banner being proudly held up by the lads saying "WHAT SOUTH DRESSING ROOM JINX?".

As the fans celebrated a vital day for our club, we retired back to the lounge having enjoyed the presentation of the trophy which was met with a massive crescendo of cheers. I was drained, albeit ready for another drink. Shortly afterwards Stuart, who had been on the pitch to present the trophy returned and came over to me in the lounge and gave me one of the Nationwide banners which said proudly, PLAY OFF FINAL WINNERS. A lovely memento which I retain to this day.

After most of the crowd had subsided it was time to leave and we got into the lift to go down to the car park. The lift though went up instead of down and when the doors opened, there was Steve Coppell and Wayne Thomas, holding the trophy. We eagerly invited them in and Wayne came right in while Steve had to be encouraged. He eventually got in with us and we dropped them off before heading down to the basement to retrieve our car.

In the basement we walked to our car and I noticed Sergei Shtanyuk. This was too good an opportunity to miss and we went over and shook his hand and spoke a little. We had time for a photo with him and it was just the end to a perfect day (almost the best day of my life! But please keep that to yourself.)

Of course Stoke being Stoke, it was not just as simple of enjoying the occasion and preparing for life in the Championship again. The victory wasn't enough for our manager Gudjon to receive the contract that he felt he had deserved and so he left the club, just as we were on the straight and narrow again. Nothing is ever straightforward at Stoke City.

CHAPTER FOURTEEN
Back in Division Two – The
Championship 2002/03

So, a new division again, up one step on this occasion so a good thing, but no manager. However in the close season it appeared that Stoke had done some really good business by recruiting Steve Cotterill who was a young, up and coming manager who had done very well at Cheltenham Town. He was their most successful manager getting them promoted into the football league and then securing another promotion in the 2001/02 season. He had earned his chance.

One issue that existed was the playing staff which had only been strengthened with one significant signing, Chris Greenacre from Mansfield Town, who had been a prolific scorer. After a slowish start we began to get our act together and secured a few good wins including an important away win at Brighton who were now playing their matches at the Withdean Stadium, which was created as an athletics stadium. I had acquired some Nationwide tickets and taken the Finance Director of a large Housing Association, Martin Heys who lived in Brighton and liked a few beers.

The facilities at the Withdean were fairly basic and the hospitality was provided in temporary accommodation. We had met in town earlier for a few beers and had a meal planned for afterwards, which usually went the way of two bottles of wine and several more beers.

Another striker had been signed, Tommy Mooney the veteran forward from Birmingham on loan and he put us in front from a first half penalty. It was difficult to see this well as we were precisely on the touchline and so only the net bulging was going to confirm a positive outcome. It did so we were on our way.

The game wasn't great and we were pleased to see half time arrive and some refreshment then settled down for the second half where we continued to press and remained solid at the back. Late on we did score a second through Andy Cooke and while there was still time for a late Brighton consolation, three good points earned. Now for a late supper and some celebratory drinks.

We followed this up with a really good performance at home to Ipswich, who would end up finishing seventh and just miss out on the play offs. I remember clearly the power in Sergei's header that gave us the lead. He didn't score many but this one was a cracker! We won through another Andy Cooke goal and took all three points in a 2 – 1 victory.

Three more solid performances followed with draws against Nottingham Forest, Reading and Crystal Palace. Then everyone was shocked to learn that Cotterill had quit the club to take over as Assistant Manager at Sunderland with Howard Wilkinson. Never in my time has an ex manager of our club received such venomous stick. He is unaffectionately known as the Quitter, or Quitterill and I wont help ease his pain. It was such a dreadful, disloyal piece of behaviour that he will have to continue to suck it up for the rest of his career, which pretty much fell apart after that despite all the early promise.

We needed a new manager fast and George Burley was the favourite and apparently was present for the midweek match versus Watford where we lost 2 – 1 at home. Perhaps he didn't like what he saw as he failed to turn up for the press conference the following day scheduled to announce his arrival at the club. Or perhaps George had indulged in a few more drinks than normal that night of the match.

Anyway this paved the way for Tony Pulis to be named manager. The Stoke support was underwhelmed, perhaps due to his ultimately acrimonious days as Gillingham manager. He took charge for our 4 – 2 drubbing at Walsall. Things didn't improve for four games until we drew at Gillingham 1 – 1 in a typical Tony Pulis performance. Clive Clarke certainly enjoyed his goal there to exorcise some of the demons from the play off semi final a few years earlier.

We needed some new players and we got them. Some senior old boys such as Paul Warhurst and Lee Mills and two others in particular who meant that we ultimately stayed up. The first was Mark Crossley the old Nottingham Forest keeper, now at Middlesborough and striker Ade Akinbiyi. Ade became an instant hit with Stoke fans, not for skill or touch, but for sheer graft, sprinting all over the place to close down the opposition and his strength; he would have made a great centre half.

Although we lost (painfully) at home to Coventry 2 – 1 we took points off Portsmouth and Wimbledon and despite a 4 – 2 reverse at Bradford on Boxing Day, a really good game actually where I was sat up in the gods in the impressive main stand at the ground. Garry, Jamie and my son Dan were with me and then we returned for the home game on 28th December to win a great game 3 – 2 against Sheffield Wednesday. The match ebbed and flowed until Brynjar Gunnarsson scored a winner after a great run from midfield in the last minute. All was feeling good with the world once again.

Come the New Year and I had a trip to Norwich to look forward to. A customer of ours the CEO of Anglia Housing Group had a box at Norwich and invited me along. I am sure he anticipated a home win and this was looking increasingly likely as we first went 1 – 0

123

and then 2 – 0 down in the first half. He celebrated each goal in the box by bashing the glass screening which shook each time he assaulted it.

We scored a good goal through Brynjar, a header this time to give us a chance and when Lee Mills shot into the top corner I enjoyed my celebration. The other occupants in the box were very humble in tolerating me until I exclaimed that we should now go and get the winner. We had been in their half three times in the game, so I think they thought I was taking the piss.

Mark Crossley's first game was away at Ipswich where I had rather foolishly bet a tenner on 0 – 0 at 15/1. There is always a good reason for the odds offered and though I knew we would keep our part of the bargain, I hoped that Ipswich might misfire. There hadn't been a 0 – 0 draw at Portman Road all season. Crossley's first piece of action was to bring down their forward in the early minutes and I feared a penalty and a sending off. Neither came as the ref saw it differently and we got away with it. After that he was inspired and saved us several times during the game which did indeed end 0 – 0.

My next away game was with a crowd of mainly Wolves fans at the Wolves v Stoke game where I was told to sit on my hands by my boss, Jeremy Wood, a fervent Wolves fan. We had enjoyed dinner before, had a few glasses and again I thought, what the hell, and bet another tenner on 0 – 0, only at 12/1 this time. Ultimately another £120 in the bank. Well done Tony, we were seeing your true colours already.

We were hanging on as the season drew to a close and a home win against Brighton 1 – 0 was a vital three points against fellow relegation candidates. In our last three games we played Coventry away. We won 1 – 0, a game I have described earlier. I took my banner, given to me at the Play Off final to this match and proudly displayed this to remind the players that we hadn't come all this way merely to be dispatched back to the old third Division. Then it was Palace away where we lost 1 – 0 and finally at home to Reading where we needed to win to stay up, or at least guarantee staying up.

Over 20,000 attended this game, Reading were safely in the Play offs and we were up for it on a hot day in early May. It was quite an atmosphere and when Ade Akinbiyi scored a near post header early in the second half, we knew we would be safe and celebrated accordingly. The players did their usual parade around the ground post match and a large number of fans stayed on to cheer them for their magnificent efforts. Afterwards it was back to Ade's until late reliving the highlights with all the lads and reveling in our survival.

2003/04 Season

Having narrowly avoided relegation we were looking forward to a full season under Tony Pulis and our first game in the bright sunshine was away at Derby. The Club had introduced ID cards to curb crowd trouble at our away matches and while this wasn't a popular measure, and one that fans had to pay for, it did the trick and away games became virtually trouble free. The deal was that you needed to produce your ID card at the away turnstiles together with your match ticket and that without it, you would be refused entrance. If there was any bother involving you, the card would be revoked and you wouldn't be able to acquire a ticket for any away match. All our away matches became ticket only, regardless of the demand that existed.

I travelled to Derby with Garry, my eldest son Dan and Jason, the dad of one of Dan's school friends who was a Derby fan. There was a large contingent of Stoke fans and we arrived in good time, met Ade and the guys and it was only then, at the ground, I realised I had left our ID cards at home. True to form they refused me and my five

125

year old son entry. I saw red and while I knew that this was the stated consequence I got riled with the steward. Ade helped intervene a bit more calmly and after speaking to a police officer who had walked over, they agreed to let us in; just this once.

I am glad they did as we went on to record a great away win 3 – 0 even though that score line flattered us a bit. It might have been quite different however as our stand in goalkeeper Ed De-Goey was involved in bringing down their striker who had rounded him in the opening minutes. Luckily the ref, Howard Webb, felt the striker had dived and booked him, it was a marginal call. Goals from Gifton Noel-Williams, Greenacre and Lewis Neal gave us the perfect start to the season. Pride Park is a neat stadium and it makes a difference to have the corners filled in unlike our ground at present.

At home to Wimbledon in our next game we went top of the league with a dramatic 2 – 1 win with a very, very late winner by Wayne Thomas. This was my youngest son, Thomas's first ever game and after the win, for a short time, we were joint top of the league.

Dan and I travelled to Walsall enroute to Bournemouth where we were holidaying the following week so we picked up the M5 and headed down a little later than my wife who had taken our youngest, Thomas with her. Carl Asaba put us ahead and while it ended 1 – 1 and was otherwise quite uneventful, it was notable for two things, first Paul Merson scored a very good equalizer, the last time I ever saw him play. The second was that we learned for sure that Paul Williams was not up to the job at centre-half.

We then struggled a bit and even lost at West Brom 1 – 0, which was a bit odd for a Tony Pulis side. Very early on there were two sending's off, John Eustace for us and Andy Johnson for them after a clash in the box that didn't seem very serious, we lost the more

126

influential player and it cost us dear. Later in the game Marcus Hall was also sent off and to be honest they were on top for most of the game.

The game away at Ipswich was televised and this was always going to be a tough game. They took the lead just before half time and we were hanging on. Late in the second half we won a penalty and Keith Andrews stepped up, his spot kick hit the right upright bounced along the line, hit the other post and bounced into the keeper's hands. Sometimes you know its just not going to be your day.

We were beginning to struggle and by the time we played Cardiff at home, we were near the relegation zone. We ended up losing 3 – 2 and while John Eustace and Ade Akinbiyi netted for Stoke, the real story were the three Cardiff goals all expertly taken by Peter Thorne who had scored a hat trick on his return to Stoke. He didn't celebrate and we all knew just what we were missing when he left us for the Bluebirds.

I was away in London midweek and enjoyed a fabulous lunch at Le Gavroche with some lovely customers to celebrate some great property deals we had completed together. That all drew to a close at about half three and I had ages to get to my hotel, get changed and then have a few beers on the way to West Ham where we hoped, but didn't expect a decent performance and result. To bolster our defence Gerry Taggart had joined us and while he didn't look totally match fit, he made such a difference organizing the defence and personally commanding the unit. We even took the lead as Frazer Richardson scored a good goal in the first half to send us all crazy in the quite busy away end terrace. We gave some stick to the usual band of West Ham fans who sat in the stand to our left. Both sides also hit the post, our effort was from John Eustace, and we saw the game out with great thanks to the role played by Gerry in the centre of defence.

127

Unfortunately I wasn't at the Brit to witness Peter Hoekstra's hat trick against Reading, showing the class that we all knew he possessed but which all too rarely was delivered.

I was enjoying taking my boys to the games now and again and Dan, being that bit older was more self sufficient. At this point Tom needed all of the equipment I could pack into my rucksack to get him through the games. We saw some good moments during this season and especially getting back to winning ways against West Brom with a resounding 4 – 1 win. They were promoted to the Premier league that season, depriving us of some certain points for a year or two.

A finish of eleventh with 66 points and amazingly a positive goal difference (not usual for Stoke City), was a reasonable outturn, especially after we had struggled for parts of the season. As for the cups, I took both sons to watch the FA Cup at fairly local Wimbledon (playing at the hockey stadium in Milton Keynes). This was just twenty minutes from home in Northampton, and we saw a poor game in the snow where we drew 1 – 1. My abiding memory from that game was the headed chance missed by Chris Greenacre near the end, a glorious chance that he somehow skied well over the bar from just a couple of yards. That meant I had to go to the replay at Stoke and this was one of the least memorable matches I had ever been to. We lost 1 – 0. Gillingham knocked us out of the League Cup and so it was all focus on the league.

2004/05 Season

We had enjoyed a good pre-season, we even beat Valencia (and were to reconvene with this major force some years later). Having beaten Wolves 2 – 1 at home on the first day of the season, we followed this up with a couple of draws and then three more wins against Gillingham and Derby at home and then Cardiff away. It all looked set for a good if not great season.

At the home game against Ipswich, a midweek affair, there was a big crowd and I had travelled to the game with my best mate Mark Webster, an Ipswich fan. He chose to join the away fans while I watched as usual in the Boothen End with the lads. It was a good game, very entertaining and in the end we got the deserved win. Ipswich had gone ahead on 41 minutes through Jason De Vos and Wayne Thomas equalized with a good header from a corner right on half time. Ipswich had the lead again early in the second half before Thomas again with another header equalized for the second time. Akinbiyi was causing a few problems, racing at defenders and really closing down the play. Eventually all his hard work paid off after a horrible mix up at the back allowing him to collect the ball and score into an empty net on 85 minutes to seal a great win. This sent us top of the league.

Then it all went a bit binary, very Tony Pulis like. I headed to Burnley for the away game on 25th September taking Garry and Jamie and my youngest son, Tom. We saw an exciting game and soon found ourselves 2 – 0 down. They had a player sent off and after Akinbiyi had pulled one back, it was all Stoke. We equalized early in the second half, Akinbiyi again with a powerful close range shot and then laid siege to the Burnley goal. The winner wouldn't come, but it was a good game, then of course a long way home. Their manager was Steve Cotterrill and as you can imagine there was some anger vented toward him, all thoroughly deserved.

Tom and I made the journey to Leicester in the rain for our next game and in an end to end encounter, we drew 1 – 1 with Carl Asaba scoring from close range. After that we had the better chances to win the game.

Our season really petered out when we lost five in a row all 1 – 0 from 28th December.

I took both of my sons to the game at Wolves on 19th March having met up with the lads on the way. We were housed in the lower seating area on the side of the pitch where the new stand was erected. It wasn't a great view and the sun was right in our eyes, however we took the lead through Gifton Noel Williams (now christened Gifton GOAL Williams). It looked as though I would eventually get to see my side win at Molineaux. That was until the final minute when they grabbed a late and not very well deserved equalizer. Our keeper was now Steve Simonsen and he made a number of good saves to keep us ahead but couldn't quite deny the very late equalizer. We went home disappointed.

More disappointment was right around the corner at home to Cardiff. Cameron Jerome scored twice and Peter Thorne (again) piled on the agony as we lost 3 – 1 with Clint Hill our scorer. The season ended with two disappointing 1 – 0 losses at home to Watford then away at Sunderland in front of 47,350 at the Stadium of Light, I didn't go to this one and they had already won the league and promotion back to the premiership.

We finished twelfth with 61 points.

The highlight of the season was probably our trip to Arsenal in the FA Cup, where at Highbury a crowd of 36,579 watched the game. There was a very large away support boisterous and loud and it was quite a party atmosphere in the Clock End. I had driven down with Garry and Jamie and also my two boys as we were being hosted by a customer who had a box above the Clock End. Ken was his name and while he couldn't attend, he saw to it that we were very well looked after. It was a great position to see the game and meant that we were very close to the away support and even picked out a few of the lads, including Garry and Jamie in the crowd below.

In a close first half where both sides created chances, we amazingly took the lead on the stroke of half time. Akinbiyi had a header saved by Lehmann and the ball fell to Thomas who absolutely slammed it into the roof of the net. Together with the travelling fans below, we went crazy on the balcony of the box. Arsenal equalized through Reyes and eventually scored again through Robin Van Persie from a Jermaine Pennant cross. We would come to appreciate his crossing ability in a few years time. We were still creating chances and before they went ahead for the first time, Akinbiyi let loose a shot from 25 yards which crashed against the crossbar with Lehmann well beaten.

It was a performance, if not a result, that everyone enjoyed. Unfortunately it didn't translate to a major uptick in league form. Sometimes you just have to remember the good moments and block the rest out, a bit like my golf. If I were to dwell on all my rubbish shots I would drive myself mad, so I just try and reflect on the ones that went well – it usually doesn't take long.

131

CHAPTER FIFTEEN 2005/06
Exit Pulis, enter Boskamp

Tony Pulis wasn't endearing himself to the Icelandic owners and refusing to play a number of the players the owners had brought to the club put a further strain on their relationship. Tony could be quite an awkward bloke, would you believe! So in the close season he was sacked and the owners brought in their own choice of new manager, Johan Boskamp. He was a very capable midfielder in his day who played for Feyenoord and was in the Dutch world cup squad in the 1978 FIFA World Cup.

The plan was to bring a more attractive attacking style to the club, quite a contrast to the Tony Pulis style and we were all about to embark on an interesting rollercoaster ride with him in charge. So we signed some players to achieve this transition, notably, Carl Hoefkens, the gifted striker Paul Gallagher (on loan), Mamady Sidibe (not sure what element of attractive passing football he would contribute toward) and Luke Chadwick who still had something to offer.

We started inauspiciously with two wins (away at Milwall then home to Luton by a single goal), two defeats and a draw. But then two away wins were welcomed first at Hull midweek. It was the usual long journey and Ade's son Max was mascot so quite a few of us decided to journey over. Hull's new stadium is impressive and the match was settled by a sharp finish by Paul Gallagher in the second half at the away fans end. We then saw the remainder of the game out comfortably. Then, away at Preston in a televised game we also won when Gallagher again scored in the 76th minute beating Carlo Nash, who was later to become a Stoke player. Again we held out for another away win. I wasn't at this match though certainly enjoyed the live coverage and had a mental of my own with my son Dan when he scored with a crisp low shot into the corner.

We then lost six of the next seven games and it appeared that we were going nowhere and nearing that destination quickly. That was followed by six wins in the next eight games where Sambego Bangoura scored in six out of seven matches. Gallagher also got four goals and we were kind of on track. Bangoura was an enigma. He could be the best striker on the planet one day and invisible the next. He had the ability to leap like a salmon for headers and possessed a great touch, he knew how to finish. He drew my attention in the 3 – 2 win at home to Leicester on 9th December. After we had gone behind, Gally leveled for us with a twice taken penalty. We fell behind again in the second half before first Sidibe scored to level with a well taken glancing header and then, Bangoura scored the winner in the 78th minute.

There were some particular highlights toward the end of the season which was drifting into a mid table skirmish again. The first memorable one was away at Portman Road, Ipswich where we sealed a stunning win 4 – 1, it was a tremendous occasion worthy of the long trip to Suffolk. We took the lead through an own goal then conceded an equalizer before half time. We were still on top and when Bangoura scored a sublime volley to make it 2 – 1, we went from strength to strength. First Luke Chadwick danced through their defence to make it 3 – 1 and then Daryl Russell, the ex Norwich player, scored a fourth to make it emphatic. I enjoyed that one, though Mark, my best friend found it harder going. Good job I knew how to celebrate in a humble way to consider his feelings (not likely, I went bananas).

In the following game at home to Southampton we went 2 – 0 down, eventually losing 2 – 1. The game was best remembered for an outstanding goal by Gally who scored a cracker from the angle of the box, a wonderful strike.

Our final game of the season saw us play away at Brighton and Dan was the Stoke mascot so there was a good contingent of the lads present again at the Withdean stadium. At this game we stayed over and Dan, Tom and Sarah were all there with me. It was a memorable day. Days out at Brighton often are worth remembering.

We arrived early and as Dan was taken to get changed and meet the players, Tom, Sarah and I had a drink in the lounge and waited to be escorted to the away fans seating area over the running track behind the goal.

Dan had a chat with Noel Blake our assistant Manager and Michael Duberry led him out. Brighton were already relegated and we took them apart. Adam Rooney scored sharply after six minutes then again after twenty two. We were in dreamland when Sidibe scored our third before half time. Rooney completed his hat trick after sixty three minutes and while they got a consolation we scored a fifth to record a memorable away win 5 – 1. We waited after the match to see the players off and Boskamp bode a humble farewell. Not knowing what chapter would unfold next, we enjoyed a good night with chips by the pier and then back to the hotel, we were all shattered.

Earlier in the season, Bangoura had left for international duty in the New Year with Guinea and decided not to return. He just went AWOL and we were all left to wonder what might have been, as I say, he was the real deal. Boskamp was asked about him in several interviews and described him as "a shit guy".

As for the cups in this season, I treated my sons to a trip to Field Mill, Mansfield in the league cup where we took the lead from a

Dave Brammer penalty in the first half, only to concede and then have to endure extra time and penalties. Our penalties in this game were pitiful, and we lost the shootout 3 – 0, we missed all our penalties. In the FA Cup I endured a home draw 0 – 0 against the mighty Tamworth and then journeyed there for the replay in which we luckily scrapped a 1 – 1 draw in the ninety minutes and it ended up with penalties again. This time everyone scored. We scored all five and they missed one. Carl Hoefkens scored the winning spot kick to send us into the next round against Premier League, Birmingham where we lost 1 – 0 at home.

CHAPTER SIXTEEN
Coates & Pulis 2006/07

At the end of the 2005/06 season the Icelandic owners had had their fill and put the club up for sale. The only serious buyer was Peter Coates who re-established ownership and reinstated Tony Pulis for the new season. Fans were a bit underwhelmed again.

Peter Coates enabled a number of new signings that would change the face of the club and help define its future. Players such as Danny Higginbotham the amazing mercurial Ricardo Fuller, (Dan's favourite player) Liam Lawrence, Rory Delap, Salif Diao, Andy Griffin and would you believe it Patrik Berger!

Our first game in the hot sunshine was at Southend and we trekked down looking forward to some points. My youngest son, Tom was mascot on this occasion and just as the last season had ended, we hoped the winning run and the omens with my son on the pitch as mascot would mean another win.

We were disappointed and didn't play at all well. We lost 1 – 0 to a Freddy Eastwood penalty, who was adjudged fouled by Steve Simonsen. We all thought the decision was debatable.

We began to find our feet and a defining moment came away at Leeds United. I dislike Leeds, not as much as Coventry, but still quite a lot. They are an arrogant lot who think they are better than they are. Let them get promoted back to the Premier League I say, so we can all kick their arse again. Anyway our defining moment came in the form of a humiliating 4 – 0 away win capped by a cracker from Ricardo Fuller for the travelling Stoke fans to celebrate.

In our next game I was entertaining customers from Manchester at the game at home to Sunderland in a Sky Box. It turned out to be a good game that we eventually and deservedly won 2 – 1. However Rory Delap was involved in a 50/50 challenge and broke his leg in two places. The club stuck by him and could have ended his loan period (from Sunderland). This was incredibly loyal by our club and which paid huge dividends in the years to come.

My sons and I enjoyed a fabulous 5 – 0 win against Norwich at home with Daryl Russell getting the last goal in a thrilling Saturday afternoon match. Then at home against Coventry City midweek I couldn't get to Stoke and watched the match in my local pub. It looked as though it would be abandoned as the fog was awful. Play continued and Andy Griffin scored a 30 yard goal that arrowed into the top corner. There weren't many people in the pub and I went completely mental as that ball went in. It was not only one of the best goals I have ever seen, but against Coventry City as well, what a night. It was the start of a five match winning streak including the regulation win against West Brom.

The away win at West Brom gave us hope of reaching the play offs as we raced into a 3 – 0 lead and eventually won 3 – 1. It all came down to the last game of the season at QPR where we needed to win to hopefully get into the playoffs (in actual fact unless we had won by a lot, we wouldn't have got there). I arrived in time for a very quick pint and then entered the low level seating at this old fashioned ground. They were one of the most cynical teams I can ever remember. They took the lead and we eventually got back in it through a Sidibe equalizer, despite him being quite badly injured a few minutes earlier. Right at the death Dominic Matteo missed a clear header right in front of us. Anyway it was a good season, we had given it a real go. We finished eighth on 73 points.

In the FA Cup Sarah, Dan, Tom and I all travelled to Fulham a Premier League side and Garry and Jamie also travelled in convoy with us. We lost 3 – 0 but we played well and gave a good account of ourselves. We were making progress!

2007/08 Season

The new arrivals for this season were a certain Ryan Shawcross and veteran Richard Cresswell. We were optimistic as usual, I have never understood those people who cant be optimistic at the start of the season, even before a ball has been kicked. We began away at Cardiff, not an easy start.

I couldn't travel to the game and celebrated from a distance when we scored with Ryan Shawcross netting for us early on. I was less joyous when Cardiff won a penalty in the last minute. However, Simonsen (Simmo) saved the penalty and we won the three points.

By now I was going to most games and my sons were with me, almost every step along the way. They hadn't just been glory hunters like me. They had undergone their initiation, their apprenticeship if you like at the more ordinary football grounds, without the opportunity to watch our heroes on match of the day or all of the publicity that accompanies the Premier League big boys. Years earlier I used to search around in the Sunday newspapers for the tiniest column, sometimes just a few sentences describing our performance. Yes, life could be very different.

The way this season unfolded has been done before, my favourite version being Stephen Foster's book *She Stood There Laughing* so I wont try and run through all the season's highs and lows, we won promotion finishing in second place.

138

I will however reflect on some personal highlights including some of the days out with my sons and what was going on at work and in the UK Property Industry at the time.

After beating Charlton a week after the win at Cardiff, we were top of the league. That's when we sometimes, if ever, get to experience these dizzy heights with the world soon collapsing and normal order resumed shortly thereafter. That's what happened with a defeat at Southampton and then three draws, including two horrible 0 – 0 stalemates at home to first Wolves and then Barnsley. We were in mid table.

For our game at Leicester at the end of September I was picking up my daughter, Sarah up from Newark and pulled in a favour to get us both into the Directors box. While I didn't know it at the time, this included a really good lunch beforehand with Milan Mandaric. This was new territory for Sarah and she enjoyed the surroundings and how incredibly polite our hosts had been. It was a tight affair and Ricky put us ahead in the first half with a good finish from twenty yards. That's how it stayed until half time. In the second half we couldn't increase our lead and eventually succumbed to an equalizer. In the lounge afterwards, Mr Mandaric wasn't too impressed with Stoke's nullifying tactics. Little did he know at that stage that his club would be getting relegated at the end of the season and we would be going in the opposite direction.

We had started to put together some useful results and the way that Ricky was playing, we always felt we had a chance in any game. The boys and I were looking forward to the home game against Sheffield Wednesday to continue our impressive run. Indeed Ricky scored twice, but unfortunately the strugglers from Sheffield scored four times. At half time it was all square at 2 – 2 as first we took the lead then went 2 – 1 down before Ricky got his second. Some interesting characters were on the pitch including Graham Kavanagh,

139

nearing the end of his career now and who crossed for their third goal. Also Deon Burton, our Millennium Stadium hero scored their fourth. In goal for Sheffield Wednesday was Lee Grant, now between the posts for the Potters after the injury to Jack Butland. My sons weren't too impressed with the result though.

In the following midweek we won away at Crystal Palace which both pleased and surprised me in equal measure. Then the wheels looked like they had fallen off with defeats by first Bristol City and then, disastrously, at home to Coventry. We would have our revenge though!

In midweek we were off to Scunthorpe with Garry and Jamie in tow. A long and ultimately worthwhile journey, though it didn't always look like that was how it was going to turn out. We were packed into the away terracing behind the goal and relieved to see Cresswell neatly score in the first half to give us the lead. We weren't in the lead for long as they equalized after just six more minutes.

It was quite even in the second half and they looked the likelier scorers. When they did score again, after eighty five minutes, it felt like another night of disappointment was on the cards. I remember their keeper running over half the length of the pitch to then slide on his knees for fifteen yards or more and give it the repeated fist pump toward the away fans.

Out of nowhere it was as though a switch had been flicked. We got forward put crosses in and from one testing cross from Danny Pugh, who had been awful up to that point, the pressure caused an own goal. We continued to press with the Stoke fans now really fired up and with seconds left, it was Pugh again with a delicate hanging cross that found Liam Lawrence on the edge of the six yard box. Liam headed accurately back across goal. We were standing right in

140

line with the trajectory of the ball as it left the keeper stranded and sailed into the bottom corner of the net to spark some really serious celebrations and some very choice words for their celebrating keeper who was now head in hands. A close win, but three more points which kept us in touch near the top.

After a 1 – 0 defeat at home to Sheffield United we went on a twelve game unbeaten run including six wins. Even during this period, I think I was realistically hoping for a solid play off place. Then of course there would be the predictable agony of another narrow defeat which would send us back down the snake, rather than up the ladder and into the Premier League. I'm not sure when the realization kicked in that it was really possible but as Hull and Bristol City were our two main rivals along with West Brom, the inkling was definitely there. We still had to play all three of them at home.

I travelled up to Bramall Lane, Sheffield United in early December and met Owen for a pre match beer. I had never seen us win at this ground. A good group of away fans, but by no means packed were behind the goal which we were attacking in the first half. First Cresswell scored well into the corner after just two minutes, the perfect start. Then we went further ahead when James Beattie (who became a very effective Stoke City player just a couple of years later) headed into his own net. We were getting the luck which had so often deserted us. Shawcross then seized on some awful defending to score from close range and less than twenty minutes in and we were 3 – 0 up. This doesn't happen often and certainly not away from home. The trip home was a good one!

So on the pitch things were looking good, we could score goals and Ricky and co were on fire. At work it was a different story as Nationwide were caught right in the centre of the Credit Crunch as first the Financial Crisis and then the recession took hold. The effect of this was for the Society's funding lines to substantially dry up (and they relied on this to fund their mortgage and Commercial Lending activities). My team had a strong pipeline of deals to complete and we were instructed to close off the pipeline and pull out of any deals where we hadn't given a firm commitment to the customers. This was incredibly hard for the business and colleagues to accept as their life blood was relationship management and doing deals. The markets hadn't adjusted fully at this stage to what was to become a full blown recession with property prices tumbling.

The business I had led for nearly ten years to build into an amazing origination engine, was being asked to operate in second gear. I began to talk to Lloyds Bank about an opportunity to join them and run a large part of their Major Corporate Real Estate business. This would mean working in London at their Gresham Street Head Office. For me this would mean either relocating South, or a big commute. However it was an opportunity to advance again, with an organization with massive reach and Corporate Lending firepower, so I was tempted. The state of affairs at Nationwide sharpened my interest.

By now I was starting to believe that Stoke could get promoted. One of the things I would miss terribly if I were to leave the Society would be the banter among all my football supporting colleagues. Across nearly eighteen years they had mercilessly taken the piss out of me. I was going to enjoy it to the full, if we could only get over the line.

Our last game before Christmas was at home to West Brom who would become the winners of the League earning automatic promotion to the Premier League. Ricky took them apart with a brilliant hat trick, his first for the club and as well as maintaining our astonishing run against West Brom, we went top of the league again.

I wasn't at the Boxing Day game at Barnsley, though I had been to Oakwell previously where we were knocked out of the FA Cup some years earlier. I am sure that any Stoke fans reading this who were there, and who stayed until the very end, will remember the game forever. We had another hat trick hero on this day and it was Liam Lawrence. Two of his goals were penalties, one in the ninety eighth minute, but even these heroics only earned us a point as Barnsley had led three times in the game.

The New Year brought Newcastle United to Stoke in the FA Cup and the expectation was high. This gave us a chance to pit ourselves against Premier League opposition. The match ended 0 – 0 with our best chance falling right at the end but the ball couldn't quite be forced over the line. So a replay at St James Park was on the cards, where I had only ever previously been to watch England play.

My office visit to my Newcastle lending team was organized for the morning after the replay at St James Park. I set off on the long journey on my own and was quietly confident about how we might perform. It was around 4pm and I was passing the Angel of the North when it happened. A BBC Newsflash that Kevin Keegan had been appointed as Manager after Big Sam Allardyce was sacked. I may as well have turned my car round and headed home. Instead of a half full stadium echoing with the sounds of Delilah, a dejected home support and a real chance for us to bag a win and progress into round four of the cup, there was an instant stampede for tickets by the Geordies. Keegan came on the radio and implored fans to attend and give the team a boost. They responded and there was mayhem around the ground as they saw the return of their own Messiah.

There were many Stoke fans at the game and despite the Keegan news, they were in pretty good spirits. All the local pubs were rammed pre-match. I had popped into one of these for a few looseners and even the scale of the endless steps up to the away seating in the very top of the main stand didn't diminish my enthusiasm. There was a great atmosphere from both sets of fans and despite losing the game 4 – 1, it remains memorable. Liam Lawrence scoring the best goal of the game after the match was effectively over at 4 – 0. Playing for Newcastle were some characters who would be representing Stoke City in the future, one of whom would score memorably for us at St James Park. First there was Shay Given in goal, who became our reserve keeper and Michael Owen, who scored their opener. Abdoulaye Faye was out for this replay, however he was to return and score the late equalizer in our away game at St James Park the following season in the Premier League in an unlikely and memorable 2 – 2 draw.

By this time at Nationwide I was talking to my boss about a basis upon which I would leave the business in a respectful and orderly manner. I wanted this to reflect the eighteen very good years I had enjoyed there (and knew that Lloyds were on the verge of offering me the role). It was all very tense and I was approaching the end of an era with the Society as the recession took hold.

Stoke meanwhile were just about continuing the good work. I say just about as in the home game against Scunthorpe we were 2 – 0 down after twenty three minutes with Martin Patterson returning to score against us in the seventh minute. It remained 2 – 0 at half time and all the expectation of three more valuable points was draining away. We got one back through Liam Lawrence after fifty three minutes and were level only ten minutes later through a superb volley from Cresswell. Just a few minutes later we were in front and rampant and were in a winning position. This after sheer disconsolation at half time where the chat in gents was a tad on the negative side! We had also returned to the top of the league.

I left Nationwide on Monday 3rd March after a pretty disgraceful meeting with my boss. The exit was neither respectful or orderly and the principles I had discussed and agreed were ignored. I still look back with great regret about that, though it did cost the organization rather more than it needed to as I was about to resign before they pre-empted things. The day before that, Stoke were on the end of a hiding at QPR after Griffin was harshly sent off early on.

We held it together however and won three of our last four games to virtually secure the promotion before we played Leicester on the last game of the season. They needed a win to stay up and we needed a point to ensure automatic promotion. That last day was a good one. It was a drizzly afternoon in the Potteries but no one minded. The boys and I were staying over and were preparing to celebrate. As it was the point from the 0 – 0 result wasn't required to secure our promotion. It was time to express all the relief and some disbelief and just celebrate.

It started to sink in the next day as plans were already in train for the Premier League and then it felt like promotion was the easy part. Now we had to garner enough points to stay in the Premier League and not fall back from where we had come from.

I had time to reflect over the whole Summer, where I played golf, enjoyed some fabulous trips and had time to properly digest the season and all the previous ones that I had been a part of. It really felt like something I and all Stoke supporters had achieved, not just the players and the club. This togetherness was to become vital in our next and future seasons as we would pit our skills against the Premier League giants. We had something, something at the Britannia Stadium that was worth several points all on its own. The spirit, desire belief and connection with the club. Stoke supporters knew precisely what their role would be in keeping Stoke City in the best league in the world.

CHAPTER SEVENTEEN
England games and Hospitality gone mad

I have never been as passionate about the National Team as I have Stoke City.

Major tournaments in the close season keep me occupied when there are no Stoke fixtures. However, even if watching England rarely got the juices flowing, I nevertheless always felt that the opportunity to watch the national team play was a privilege.

Nationwide paved the way for opportunities to attend England matches when they extended their sponsorship of football from the EFL to the National team in 1998 after the 16th World Cup hosted in France. This was the World Cup where England reached the Round of 16 stage and lost out on penalties against Argentina after a thrilling 2 – 2 draw where Michael Owen scored that stunning goal after a great run and shot. The game where Beckham stupidly got himself sent off.

It seemed quite an opportune time to sponsor the team. We had enjoyed a reasonable Finals and the popular Kevin Keegan had taken over from Glen Hoddle.

To extract the greatest value from the sponsorship, it was essential that the team qualified for the major competitions, failure to do so would be a big dent in the exposure and PR the sponsors hoped to extract. The Euros of 2000 were being staged in Belgium and the Netherlands. England scraped through in second place to qualify, miles behind Sweden and on goal difference from Poland in third place.

World Cup qualification for the Finals in South Korea and Japan was nervy for a while. We had a relative straightforward group with Germany being the exception. They beat us in the early qualifier at Wembley, the last ever game at old Wembley.

My business area contained many of the high net worth individuals who were customers in their capacity as Property Investors in the Real Estate sector. This meant we had a strong business case when bidding to obtain hospitality tickets. Consequently we received good allocations for most games.

The hospitality was very good and the customers enjoyed the experience, even if I couldn't get as worked up about it.

One of the first games I went to was a home friendly at the old Wembley against France in February 1999. Nicolas Anelka was on fire and only denied a hat trick in a 2 – 0 win for France with a penalty that crashed against the bar. England were made to look poor against the World Cup champions. Our seats were in an area called the Olympic Grandstand, a narrow ring of seats at the very top of the stadium which were incredibly high up and gave an excellent view, not something you got from every seat in the old stadium.

I was also at the home friendly against Argentina on 23rd February 2000 and was having a great time with our guests prior to the game. We all made our way to our seats when shortly before kick off there was a stadium announcement. So somber was the announcement it was obviously news about the passing of someone important. There seemed a time delay and I had to have a double take as it was announced that Sir Stanley Matthews had died.

The noise in the whole stadium just stopped. The world seemed to stop and I felt as though I had lost a family member. I was stunned. The game became inconsequential now, it was an unattractive 0 – 0 draw. My drive home was filled with thoughts and memories of this iconic superstar and gentleman who none of us would ever get the chance to meet again.

My next game, also at the old Wembley was the last match ever played there. The weather was horrible and Germany were the opponents. It was another poor performance after all the hype and we lost 1 – 0, with Hamman firing in from distance. This all led to a very disconsolate Kevin Keegan resigning and he was superseded by Sven Goran Erikson.

After that, the England Internationals did the rounds and were played at mainly the larger venues around the country. This was a successful and popular interim measure and the atmosphere generated was far more intimidating than usually the case at Wembley.

Sven's first game in charge was against Spain at Villa Park and it was a great occasion marked by a solid 3 – 0 win. My Midlands customers loved the opportunity to watch England play locally.

I attended matches at St James Park, Old Trafford and a friendly against Croatia played at Portman Road. The games and especially the pre and post match entertainment in Manchester and Newcastle at the World Cup qualifier against Albania (St James Park) and the Euro qualifier against Liechtenstein (Old Trafford), were memorable.

The 2004 Euros were looming. Together with a very good customer I, along with friend and colleague Dave (Chalky) White, arranged to spend a couple of days in Lisbon and watch England play France, one of the tournament favourites. After leading for most of the match, David James made two spectacular rickets and in the final knockings we contrived to lose the match 2 – 1. I think this was the spark for me to get more into following England. I was even more gutted later in the tournament when England lost to Portugal on penalties in the quarterfinals, as I had secured the allocation of 4 hospitality tickets for the semi finals which we never got to see.

I had promised Ade a ticket to the semi final, so he was also gutted. However I kept my part of the bargain and sent him the ticket that we would never be able to use – unusually they had been printed and I had them sitting in my greasy hand as we were knocked out.

I don't know when it started to get out of hand, perhaps it already had. By the start of 2005, with markets booming and Real Estate funders competing tooth and nail for the same clients to further their business, corporate hospitality had lost its sense of proportion. The market became highly competitive and interest margins and fees had tumbled over the last couple of years.

The major lenders in the sector, RBS and HBoS were offering even finer terms and conditions and extravagant hospitality opportunities that were irresistible to customers. Not that we at Nationwide didn't work hard to compete.

Traditional events such as golf days or tickets to Rugby Internationals, became full day off-roading experiences or overseas trips for sporting events. At one off-road driving event the Finance Director of one of our customers was in a car that rolled on to its roof, driven by our own Divisional Director of Commercial!

Nationwide had something unique to offer and used the England team sponsorship to take "special" customers to overseas trips to watch England play, wherever that might be. I had my eye on a friendly being organized in Chicago against the USA and managed to get hold of four tickets for this rare opportunity in May 2005. It was a long way to travel for a friendly, but a very good trip and we were joined by sets of people from the other sponsors also taking customers to the match. We also had a special guest with us, Alan Ball. I have already spoken about making my peace with him over a Glenmorangie in the bar on one of the nights.

We saw a good game which England won with two good goals from Kieran Richardson and while USA pulled one back through Clint Dempsey, England were in solid control throughout. A long night followed, then a long flight home but we all figured it was worth it and remember the experience fondly.

Despite the competitive market, work was going well at this point, the property market in the UK remained buoyant, unhealthily buoyant as it turned out, and we were underwriting record new business levels.

We had our eye on the forthcoming World Cup in Germany and were planning to take various groups of customers to the group games. As you would expect these were very costly trips but we had secured the budget and of course the customers lapped it up.

I was due to take customers to the Paraguay game in Frankfurt but pulled out as my youngest son needed a medical procedure and I passed on to some very grateful colleagues. Tom's operation was completely successful and I watched the game with my son in hospital where I stayed overnight with him.

Later in the group stage I did manage to go to a game where we played Trinidad and Tobago in a hot and sunny Nuremburg. They had Kenwynne Jones playing up front and for England Peter Crouch was leading the line. Little did I know that the two key strikers on the pitch that day would be playing and scoring goals for Stoke City only a few years later in the Premier League. We won 2 – 0 and had a good night, but not as late at the evening before which was mental.

The hospitality surrounding the game was superbly organized. Security was fairly tight and on entering the hospitality area I was called to one side where they searched my small ruck sack. They pulled out my England Flag, bearing my sons names DAN and TOM in the top left and right quarters and SCFC in the bottom left. In the bottom right corner it was blank save for a Nationwide logo, and it was this that attracted their attention. I was advised I could only enter with the flag if the logo was removed. I agreed and the security man produced a large hunting knife from his belt and went about mutilating my flag.

I had really got into the World Cup and felt we could win in. We had qualified for the last 16 and were grateful for being pitched against Ecuador in the draw. We won 1 – 0 and now it was the quarterfinals in Gelsenkirchen which was just too tempting to resist. Together with the same customer who had entertained us in Lisbon, we shared the cost to splash out on a package for eight of us to attend the match.

The stadium was amazing and on this occasion, with the temperature thirty plus degrees outside, the roof was closed which built the atmosphere further. We had enjoyed the morning in Dusseldorf and around the stadium and had great seats high up and a brilliant view. The national anthem was sung with real feeling and the level of expectation was high and rising.

Unfortunately the game did not live up to any of these expectations. Portugal were quite limited in what they attempted and England were sterile and the game flowed without any real opportunities. It was hard to believe how pedestrian the game had been when Rooney kicked out at Ronaldo and was sent off (not dis-

151

similarly to his ex Manchester United colleague David Beckham against Argentina all those years earlier). Just as Beckham cost us the game then, Rooney did so on this occasion. The game drifted and while England were better with only 10 men on the pitch, the inevitable extra time and penalties approached.

I don't need to rehearse the penalties. We scored just one of our penalties and lost the shoot out 3 – 1. We were out. It was a great chance missed. Thanks Wayne.

I lost some interest and passion in following England after that and our performance in subsequent tournaments has been dire. The hospitality bandwagon kept on rolling and became even more ridiculous. I enjoyed the events and occasions, but really, looking back it was over the top. Hospitality on this scale almost completely disappeared as the market crashed and as the Bribery Act 2010 came into force on 1st July 2011.

My final example of hospitality gone mad was of a skiing trip which we organized to Verbier, Switzerland in March 2007. I attended with my Manchester team and a group of their customers. It was my first ever ski trip. It was spectacular and cost an absolute bomb. I was scheduled to leave a day early so I could get back to Geneva and fly to Barcelona to watch England play Andorra. This was a Euro qualifier and it seemed a good idea to spend a few days in sunny Barcelona after the snowy slopes of Verbier.

It didn't really work out like that. I had rushed over from Geneva and it was raining hard in Barcelona. The match was not being played at the Camp Nou, Barcelona's wonderful ground, but in the Olympic Stadium, a pretty run down, unimpressive stadium. England won 3 – 0 but in truth were very poor and Steve McLaren took some dreadful stick. It continued to rain.

I had been away for over a week now, hopping between European destinations and was glad to get home. I think I realized how nuts this had all become.

When the inevitable adjustment in the Property Market came it was overdue. The combination of a market with its brakes on, looming recession and a credit crunch meant that the Banks that had become so eager to cut margins and compete, were now braking with both feet. From a position of managing a growing business, it was time to retrench, hunker down and then the inevitable issues arose in the form of impairments (losses on lending as inflated property prices settled much lower and rent levels collapsed). Tenants were defaulting and it was about to become very messy.

CHAPTER EIGHTEEN
Joining Lloyds and the Premier League

I had been headhunted to join Lloyds in 2007. Headhunted sounds a bit grand, I received a phone call from a recruitment agency in London asking if I would like to go for a chat with a few senior guys at Lloyds about a potential opportunity. After several meetings in London it didn't lead to anything, initially.

One of the people I met was Mark Stokes, an impressive Managing Director of Large Corporates within the Corporate Bank. As the name suggests this was dealing with customers who were large corporate enterprises. Mark was interested in my background as Lloyds had accumulated a high penetration of lending in the Housing Association sector, a sector I had introduced them to years earlier. He was keen to introduce some new leadership into that team and also coordinate the Real Estate lending activity that Lloyds had rapidly become engaged in. Signs were already suggesting there was going to be a slowdown and most likely an adjustment of commercial property values.

The Real Estate lending was being transacted within the regional areas of Large Corporate, all themselves very sizeable businesses, managed by Regional Managing Directors. Real Estate was being used to grow lending and deliver fees and income, at a time when opportunities were narrowing across other parts of the business. Lloyds needed a Real Estate specialist, rather than a Generalist Corporate Manager to coordinate this lending and that's where I came in.

After more than a dozen meetings with Human Resources, Credit function, many other Managing Directors and a full day of testing with an external assessment agency, I agreed to join. I started in September 2008 based at Lloyds Head Office at 25 Gresham Street. Nationwide and I had mutually parted company earlier in that year in March, which gave me the luxury of the whole Summer off. A rare and fabulous opportunity.

2008/09 Season

Just a few weeks before I started work at Lloyds the new season, our first ever in the Premier League took off. The anticipation had been growing for several weeks since the fixtures were announced towards the end of June. It was difficult to know which match caught the eye more than the others as they were all mouth watering games. Of course fixtures against the big guns became very eagerly awaited as we had been deprived of those occasions for so long.

It was an intimidating prospect and I was trying to gauge where we could possibly pick up enough points to stay up. I did my own version of a full season prediction league, and prioritized home games and those against the fellow promoted sides and other bottom half of the table teams to seize the points we needed. Both the other promoted clubs West Brom (thank the Lord for West Brom) and Hull City were prime targets. We ended up securing ten points from our four games against these teams with three wins and a draw. This was almost a quarter of our entire points haul for the season and was crucial.

Our first game away at Bolton looked tough, but also relatively winnable if we could recapture the same intensity that had served us well in the previous season. Also, we had a few new faces in our ranks, some I wasn't so sure about and others I knew would be a hit

155

right from day one. Dave Kitson was my biggest doubt while Danny Higginbotham and Abdoulaye Faye were my nailed on favourite signings. A few others were to surprise me like Thomas Sorensen and his amazing record of saving penalties.

I travelled to Bolton with Garry and we were housed in the upper tier of the stand behind the goal, as you would expect it was a large, noisy following. Nerves were soon jangling even though we went close through Leon Cort and Kitson. Bolton's first goal, a cross which sailed in, set the scene and they scored twice more before half time. Fundamentally it was all over though we battled on and Ricky scored a very good header to give us our first Premier League goal, albeit a consolation.

I think we were philosophical enough to move on accept the defeat and hope for better fortunes against Aston Villa at home the following weekend. Paddy Power had other ideas and announced they would be paying out on all bets that had been placed on Stoke being relegated. This after just that one match at Bolton and with all the season to follow. Stoke fans were incensed.

It wasn't so long ago that league tables weren't even printed in the papers until at least three or four games had been played, now after day one of the season the tables aren't just available, they are used to create judgments about who will finish in the top four and who will be relegated. And Stoke City were in the firing line already.

So, after all the headlines, the Paddy Power hysteria and hype, we moved on to our first home game in the Premier League. Aston Villa were Midlands rivals and seasoned Premier League campaigners. They possessed pace and power in their forward line, a combination we feared. This would be a tough challenge in our first home game. The Britannia crowd were so up for this game, played in bright sunshine and both my sons were there to witness what would be our first win and points of the season. Half an hour in and we are awarded a penalty which Liam Lawrence scored confidently, even though we could hardly bare to watch. The relief was obvious and the celebration lasted for ages.

I cant remember precisely when Rory Delap perfected the use of those long, flat missile like throw ins. These were more dangerous than most corners due to the angle and the trajectory and he certainly employed them regularly in this game. Rory had possessed a long throw for some time but it was at Stoke under Tony Pulis that this weapon was fully exploited. It was a unique weapon and one that has never been equaled.

It was around fifteen minutes or so into the second half when they equalized after a neat move which John Carew executed and now we faced a major test. We needed some magic, some Jamaican magic. Soon Ricky turned the experienced Laursen brilliantly and while I thought he had taken the ball to too tight an angle, he found the net with an amazing finish. We had the lead again.

Two minutes later Villa were level once again and as we were now in the last five minutes, I think most of us were thinking about banking hard earned point from the game. The fans to their credit raised the volume and really got behind the team for the final push. We won a throw in and Rory was about to deliver. The box was crowded with all eleven Villa players and most of the Stoke team as Rory launched the missile. Somehow among all the chaos, Mamady Sidibe got the important touch, the slightest of touches to glance the ball past Friedel and in the net. We had won 3 – 2. It was an amazing climax and I was doubting I could cope with this all season long. It was right to celebrate, enjoy the moment, all sorts of crap could be right around the corner!

157

My second away game was at Anfield, where we bravely held out for a 0 – 0 draw and a point that felt every bit as good as the victory against Villa. In between these two games we had lost twice.

Three more vital points came against Spurs at home. They had two men sent off and even though Ricky's very late penalty had hit both posts before rebounding out and which Rory had then smashed against the bar, nothing would deny us.

I had only ever been to the dilapidated Maine Road to watch Man City play, so the chance to visit the City of Manchester Stadium was compelling. I didn't enjoy the experience. Robinho scored a hat trick in their 3 – 0 win and the lower terrace where most away fans are housed was in the open. The view was at best average and it was raining hard in Manchester. I was glad to tick this ground off my list.

For our next home game in midweek against Sunderland, both my sons were mascots. I had picked up Sarah and we were all staying over in Stoke and had enjoyed a good day at Alton Towers on a very cold Autumn afternoon. We watched the game from the front of the main John Smiths stand and from a Rory long throw Ricky headed in halfway through the second half to give us the goal that won the game.

Just three days later it was the might of Arsenal visiting the Britannia. There was a real bear pit atmosphere, the kind of backing that won us the loudest fans in the Premier League accolade. We didn't need the artificial noise that Leicester City encourage. A famous victory followed, again from two long throws that caused mayhem in their penalty area as we bullied them into a 2 – 1 submission. This was precisely the intensity and commitment we needed to stay in the league and we were now nicking points off the big guns as well as our lower half of the table peers.

It was from this game that Arsene Wenger described Stoke as a "Rugby team", accusing us of heavy handedness and too physical an approach. So when we sing Swing Low and when we score the first goal and sing "1 – 0 to the Rugby team", that's where it all started.

We were a bit rough and the fans loved it, we had an edge and stayed just inside the limit of the rules. Arsenal always reacted the worst. Some teams handled it far better and gave as good as they got.

Because it was our first year in the league (and none of us knew if it might be our last!) Sarah, Tom, Dan and I travelled to Manchester for the game at Old Trafford. We had booked an overnight stay and were looking forward to a special occasion. It was special, but not in the way we hoped. Ronaldo got some serious stick, but also scored two exquisite goals from free kicks as we lost 5 – 0. I have been back most seasons since and still hope to watch my team get a win there one day, its been a long time since Alan Bloor scored the late winner in a 1 – 0 win in 1976.

We beat West Brom at home (of course) and after a draw at home to Hull, faced Newcastle away. I couldn't go but a number of the lads did. Our two late goals including Abdoulaye Faye's last minute equalizer earned us a draw. I was jealous I hadn't been there and enjoyed watching the highlights and Abdoulaye's celebration on MoTD.

We were holding our own and in the New Year the arrivals of Matty Etherington and striker James Beattie gave everyone a lift. My first ever trip to White Hart Lane with David (Moley) Jones, a Spurs fan, was a 3 – 1 defeat, the highlight being a really well taken goal by Beattie, his first for the club.

Next up Man City at Stoke and one of the best atmospheres ever and a performance that matched that completely. Rory was harshly sent off in the first half and we were really up against it. Despite the odds we managed to take the lead late on in the first half when a pin point cross from Etherington was met perfectly at the back post by Beattie who scored with a wonderful header. Mentals had gone up a gear or two with that one!

Now we had to hold on for forty five minutes and while they had almost all of the possession, the crowd really responded. From around seventy minutes played, the atmosphere was lifted to new heights as we backed the lads against incessant pressure. This was gutsy and another famous victory was secured.

Our victory at West Brom was our first ever away win in the Premier League. Six points against Tony Mowbray's team and such a shame that they would be relegated. We would need to replace these points in the following season. Our second away win in the Premier League would follow at Hull with two stunning goals and our survival was secure. That was quite a relief and even though we beat Wigan at home in our final home game which meant party time, our last game of the season was at Arsenal, not somewhere you want to be heading in need of points to stay up.

24th May 2009, the day of the Arsenal game was also my wedding day. I wanted it to be the brilliant, relaxed, happy marvelously sunny day that it turned out to be. It was a fantastic day (even though we lost 4 – 1 at Arsenal). The wedding day itself was a gathering of family and a few close friends, and Sinead (my wife) and I had arranged for a garden party the following day, Bank Holiday at our home. This was another glorious day and the garden was full of family and friends, including all my Stoke mates on their way back from Arsenal the day before. A great day.

In the cups we lost embarrassingly at Hartlepool in the FA Cup, pleasing Jeff Stelling on Sky Sports. In the League Cup we let ourselves down in a 1 – 0 reverse at home to Derby in the Quarter Finals.

CHAPTER NINETEEN
Banking Crisis and Staying Up

Back at the Bank the merger or more accurately the Lloyds takeover of HBoS completed in February 2009. It all started in a friendly enough manner with very senior Managing Directors and Executive Main Board members briefing all the various Divisions. We were assured that Lloyds had done its due diligence and knew what it was getting. This turned out to be patently untrue and especially in the Real Estate area, where Bank of Scotland had acquired an overweight, overleveraged, underpriced market share.

While I was at Nationwide it took some time to understand how HBoS were winning as much business as they were. Customers wouldn't disclose the detailed terms offered but consistently told us that HBoS were offering far more leverage, that is, higher level of loan to value lending.

In attempts to retain market share and returns, they stretched the traditional "Senior" debt element up to around 80%. As other lenders followed suit, they extended their offer to include "Mezzanine" funding taking the debt to over 90%. Interest margins on this Mezzanine debt were higher but it was more risky and had less rights in an enforcement than Senior debt.

They weren't finished. They saw customers making huge profits as they acquired property, saw the value rise and then sold the assets. They wanted a piece of that action too. So as well as Senior and Mezzanine debt, they additionally offered to lend a proportion of the investor equity to benefit from the higher returns when assets are sold.

This was all well and good until prices crashed, by an average of 46% from its peak across Commercial Real Estate markets. This instantly wiped out any value in both equity and Mezzanine elements. Even the Senior debt was only partly recoverable. It was a disaster largely caused by greed.

As the market shifted, we were all about to feel the pain which not only brought HBoS to its knees but, without the State Aid and Government bailout, would have bankrupted Lloyds. Their 250 year history as a largely prudent, safe and almost *boring* institution was under serious threat.

The first casualties are never the ones who deserve it most. I was leading a sizeable part of the Real Estate team as Director of Large Corporate Real Estate. This covered everything South of Manchester. The Midlands, Wales, London the South East and the rest of the South and South West. A massive change programme was being introduced which would mean carnage for the majority of colleagues.

As an example of the scale, the front line relationship teams operating throughout the Midlands (which spanned across to East Anglia and South as far as Milton Keynes) had 103 colleagues working in several regional offices. Within less than a year this team comprised of just three colleagues based in Birmingham. This pattern was repeated across the UK. It was a major leadership challenge and while my strong preference was to be building teams and businesses, I had to play a lead role in dismantling this one.

Some colleagues moved into other areas of the bank including what we called BSU (Business Support Unit). This was the intensive care and Recoveries unit for failing Real Estate lending. This was partly due to the market shift and partly because of the reckless lending undertaken by Bank of Scotland and in particular a couple of teams operating from their Headquarters in Edinburgh who took huge punts with the banks capital.

The changes continued and by the end of Stoke City's first ever year in the Premiership many of the senior Directors, including some of those who has assured us that Lloyds had done its homework, had departed.

The share price had plummeted, many Lloyds colleagues blamed their HBoS counterparts. They felt a personal grievance, especially those who had accumulated a large shareholding in the bank where they had worked for all their career. Their trust and confidence in the combined new Lloyds Banking Group was shattered.

It wasn't fun commuting to London on the daily 6.42am train often to face another wave of issues appearing in what was defined as the *Good Loan Book*. The media pounced on the collapse and negative headlines appeared daily which gave bankers very bad press.

But I was looking forward to the new season, a big one for us.

2009/10 Season

So, we stayed up, and now the really hard work began. All I was hearing was "second season syndrome" where apparently its harder to stay in the league for that second season than the euphoric first campaign. Not a bit of it. We were Stoke City and life is never easy, we all knew what to expect and hoped for two things. Firstly, that we could capitalize on the fact we had stayed up in year one and attract a few more even better players to the club, and secondly, to perform with the same intensity and do it all over again!

The crowd at the Brit were certainly up for it again. We started at home to Burnley who had just been promoted and I was invited by Brendan Flood, their Director to join him at the match. I was interested to visit the Chairman's Suite at the ground and it was good to see Bren again. He was having a ball, having personally backed the club financially and supported their promotion to the Premier League. He was now going to milk every minute of it, for however long it lasted.

At the pre match lunch we weren't on Peter Coates table. I was with Bren and were sitting next to Tony Pulis' family, his wife and daughter and we enjoyed a very nice lunch. They were really good company and after a few glasses of wine Tony's wife was telling us what Tony thought of Phil Brown, Hull City Manager. Suffice to say there was no love lost. Brown was known by many as the Tango man and was almost orange in skin colour. It remained very relaxed over lunch and Bren was quite happy for me to enjoy the occasion as a Stoke fan, rather than masquerading as a Burnley Director (unlike the Garry Gibson episode at the Vic against Hartlepool).

We went 2 – 0 up in the first half, the eventual score and it was a relaxed and controlled start to the season. At half time we were back in the lounge having a cup of tea and in came Alex Ferguson and Mike Phelan. They both exchanged pleasantries with Peter Coates and stayed for a couple of photos and seemed very happy with life, obviously the red wine was to their liking!

We had made quite a statement during the transfer window with some important signings. The highest profile had been Tuncay Sanli and Robert Huth from Middlesborough. Tuncay was the one that fans were most excited about, but Huth was the real bargain and became a rock at the back for us along with his partner Ryan Shawcross. We also added Dean Whitehead in the midfield who had

165

a good engine and was a very tough tackler, important ingredients to gaining popularity at Stoke.

The introduction of Huth and Tuncay definitely had an impact and after a few narrow defeats against top teams, Chelsea and Man Utd at home, a hard fought away win came at Everton thanks to a Robert Huth header. We repeated this at Spurs where we managed to stay in the game at 0 – 0 before Glen Whelan scored a cracker near the end to give us a valuable and famous victory.

We were fluctuating between losses and the odd win which meant we were holding our own in the league table. And we continued this into the New Year with a stunning first half performance at home against Fulham. We held a deserved 3 – 0 lead at the break and while it got a bit nervy in the second half, we saw it out and bagged another priceless three points.

At our next home game against Liverpool I was accompanied by my brother in law Brendan and his fiancé (now wife) Sian, both Liverpool fans. We conceded through a scrambled goal by Kyrgiakos which seemed a bit unfair as we had done really well up to that point. With time running out we managed a very late equalizer through Huth at the back post who gleefully hammered the ball in from close range after a mix up from a corner. So we escaped with another point. Always good to nick one off the Scousers, or anyone really.

In the FA Cup We had disposed of now non league York City and then Arsenal in a thriller at home which we deservedly won 3 – 1. We started fast and went 1 – 0 up after another Rory long throw was netted by Ricky. They equalized with a deflected goal and it was game on. However we were not to be denied as first Ricky headed a second goal from a Sidibe cross and then Dean Whitehead scored the third which killed the game off. Great celebrations and again the Britannia curse had done for the Gunners.

Our reward for these heroics was an away tie at Manchester City. Thanks a lot I thought. It barely gets tougher than this and we were up against it from very early on after a mix up at the back between our keeper and Shawcross presented Shaun Wright-Phillips with an open goal tap in.

I wasn't at the game as my wife and I had escaped to Spain for a few days but in one of the local bars I found a live screening of the game and had a beer or two as I watched us concede early. I couldn't really see us getting back into the game, though at 1 – 0 there is always a chance.

In the second half, we were awarded a throw not far into the Man City half. Rory launched a really big one, not quite as flat as the exocets, but very effective and Ricky had left his marker and scored with a powerful and well placed header. I naturally went bananas in the bar and while it was a bit nervous toward the end we earned a replay that we thoroughly deserved. Now they had to come to the Brit!

Work commitments meant I didn't get to the replay either and instead was holed up at the Hilton in Cardiff where I was meeting customers and performing an office visit with my team there.

In an amazing performance we blew Man City away. I had predicted this and shared my vision with a few Man City fans who, like me and my sons had been staying overnight for the Premier League meeting with City a week earlier. It seemed like a fixture backlog all against the same team!

In this league game we were reduced to ten men in the second half but still took the lead through Glen Whelan who fired a powerful low shot right into the corner past the helpless Hart. They did equalize and we should have won the game as Ryan scored from a corner with a great header only for this to be chalked off for a foul. Replays suggested there was no foul and that's when I told the Man City lads in the hotel bar that next time they were in town, they wouldn't get away with it so easily. And they didn't.

It wasn't all going swimmingly. I said that Man City away was about as hard a cup draw as you could get. Wrong. We drew Chelsea away in the Quarter Finals. I was invited by some customers to join them in their double sized box for the game. I have described this match earlier in the book. We limped out of the cup 2 – 0 and that's where I met Peter Bonetti.

Further euphoria and heartache combined followed as we played Arsenal at home, always feisty and fuelled by Wenger's continuing jibes about our playing style. We took the lead in trademark fashion from a Delap long throw from which Danny Pugh scored. They equalized through Bendtner just before half time. The second half is more widely remembered for the terrible leg fracture that Aaron Ramsey sustained after a miss-timed challenge by Ryan Shawcross. Ryan had been selected as part of the England squad earlier the same day and was sent off for the challenge. The injury was horrific and was amplified over and over again in the slow motion replays that got played on Sky and MoTD all evening.

In his anger, Wenger made some disgraceful comments about what was a miss-timed but honest challenge and he is a big part of the reason for the angst which exists between our two clubs. Ryan made a genuine attempt to get the ball, it was miss timed and he was slightly pulled back by an Arsenal player just before making the challenge which delayed him by those fractions of a second that make all the difference. Ramsay is playing again now and while he may feel he has some unfinished business, his general conduct in matches against us since has been very immature.

Wins against Hull at home and Fulham meant we were relaxed in mid table though losing 4 – 0 at Man Utd on the final day wasn't a great way to sign off in a televised match. We had fairly comfortably navigated our second season in the Premier League.

More turmoil at Lloyds.

Back at the bank heads were still rolling including my boss Ceri who was finding it pretty intolerable and understandably threw in the towel. She was replaced by Stuart Winton whose agenda was to implement another restructure and save further headcount in the process. Stuart was tough, ruthless and executed his instructions. I didn't like his style nor approach. The level of arrogance and lack of humility he displayed was unnecessary.

In this restructure, which involved even more office closures, both I and my co Managing Director and friend, Gary Gerrard, who looked after the North and Scotland, were displaced. It was an ugly restructure and was as unkind to customers in equal measure to the colleagues who lost their jobs.

Stuart's right hand henchman was Laura Milligan. She had been PA to Peter Cummings, Executive on the main Board of HBoS. Many people regarded him as the architect of the overstretching of the bank. Laura saw him as him as a visionary. Utter crap. She was a very nasty piece of work and in banking, like most things, what goes round comes around and eventually it came around to her getting the sack too. Good riddance.

I owe Laura one piece of thanks. She was negligent in ignoring over two thousand smaller customer accounts (loans, current accounts and deposit accounts) in her calculation for the level of staffing necessary to manage the remainder as she saw through the

169

recommendation to cut resources to the bone. It became obvious that the team could never manage this legacy portfolio and I was retained to engineer the migration of these accounts to a new home in the SME team within the bank. So in a strange way she, through her cock up, enabled me to stay in a role.

Leading the project to migrate these two thousand "unwanted" accounts to a new home was a real challenge. I agreed to take this on as well as be the lead for the Integration Project for Real Estate. This was the process of merging the several thousand client accounts from both HBoS and Lloyds together onto one system, the largest integration that had taken place in UK banking history. It wasn't fun, but an interesting experience.

Stuart bit the dust eventually, as they all do. After the portfolio of accounts had been safely transferred to SME, there was a bun fight for the remaining good Real Estate customers. These included many of the customers I was in charge of when I first joined the bank. A decision was made to transfer these customers back to the control of my original boss, Mark Stokes who had navigated his way through the changes and established a high performing business. He asked me to stay on for a bit longer and I became Interim Managing Director of the Real Estate teams in his Mid Markets business. I had gone full circle, and was glad to be back even if it was on a temporary basis.

CHAPTER TWENTY
Establishing ourselves and FA Cup Heroes

When it was time for the new season to take off, our third in the Premier League, I was up and ready for it as were my two sons. My career might have needed major surgery, but Stoke City were in good shape. We had signed Kenwynne Jones and John Walters as new strikers and Jermaine Pennant also joined to give us extra width. In goal was Asmir Begovic, a fabulous and imposing young Bosnian keeper.

On a sunny afternoon we opened the season at Wolves, Kenwynne making his debut and hitting the bar early on, before falling awkwardly and having to be substituted. The anti climax of it all. Wolves were better than us and went 2 – 0 up before Abdoulaye scored a powerful header to give us some hope. It wasn't to be and we went on to lose the next two games as well, firstly at home to Spurs where Gareth Bale did his CV no harm with both goals including a worldie to make it 2 – 1 with a waist high volley from an almost impossible angle twelve yards out. It flew into the top corner and was a goal in a million.

It was Chelsea away next and we all feared the worst after we had lost there 7 – 0 the season before. They won an early penalty which the reliable Lampard was about to take, however Thomas Sorensen made a great save to add to his penalty saving records. Sorensen had developed his own method to fool the penalty taker into believing his weight was on one side of his body only to switch at the last minute and make numerous saves from the spot. Unfortunately we still lost and that was three in a row, our worst start to a season in the Premier League.

We improved though and Kenwynne got into the groove. On his day, rare though they turned out to be, he was totally unstoppable. I took the boys to West Ham in the League Cup and an overnight stay in London during half term. It was a balmy evening and a reasonable following of Stokies who were making quite a racket and even more so when we took the lead from a Kenwynne header. When they equalized toward the end of the game through Scott Parker, it was going to be a long hard road as Pulis had withdrawn our strikers in favour of defensive players to protect our narrow advantage. We ended up losing 3 – 1 in extra time. Still a good night and a taste of Upton Park for my sons.

If October proved a tough month for us, November was the opposite three wins and a draw including a cracker 3 – 2 against Birmingham. This included probably the best goal I ever saw Ricky score. He collected the ball in his own half, got to the corner of the box and was shown to the left, his weaker foot, before curling a sublime shot into the top corner. Next was a strangely comfortable win at home to Liverpool with both Ricky and Kenwynne on the score sheet. Then at West Brom, a Birmingham based customer and complete gentleman, Keith Bradshaw, invited my sons and I to his box where we saw a rampant performance and a 3 – 0 win, easily our best away win in the Premier League. In truth we were a bit flattered but nevertheless a hugely enjoyable victory against our most generous of local rivals.

From the start of this season I had managed to get hold of the tickets for the two boxes that the Bank had contracts on for the games against Stoke. One was at The Emirates and the second at Old Trafford. It was the last year the bank maintained these facilities and too good an opportunity to miss, so I invited the lads from Stoke to make up the numbers with me first at the Old Trafford game where we enjoyed a few drinks and a good pre-match dinner. We also celebrated as Dean Whitehead equalized for us, although still ended on the losing side 2 – 1.

At The Emirates I also had the luxury of the bank box and friends, contacts and my two sons enjoyed a good evening albeit a narrow 1 – 0 defeat. Jermaine had a free kick chance in the last few minutes at our end but couldn't quite squeeze it in. This was the game that was postponed due to heavy snow, while we were minutes from the ground.

We enjoyed some stunning results toward the end of the season including a thumping 4 – 0 at home to Newcastle, 3 – 0 demolition of Wolves and the most impressive, a 3 – 1 display against Arsenal who were simply outplayed. During these games we did suffer some injuries with Matty Etherington and Robert Huth on the treatment table and Danny Higginbotham unfortunately receiving a long term injury to deprive him of an FA Cup Semi and Final appearance. We finished the season in a safe thirteenth place on Forty Six points.

However, the real story of the season was our FA Cup run where Cardiff were our opponents at home in round three. We made hard work of this and drew 1 – 1 at home. I re-organized my work diary and made it down to Cardiff for the replay where the initial ninety minutes were disappointing and ended 0 – 0. Extra time, that neither team wanted brought us relief as John Walters scored twice, the first a header, to seal the win.

I was determined to go to all our FA Cup games this year and had my tickets for Wolves away in the next round. To thwart me, the game was moved from Saturday to the Sunday and even though I had hold of the tickets, I just couldn't go. I was driving while we were playing and it was tense stuff. Huth had given us a lead and Stoke fans who made up what seemed the majority of the 11,967 crowd were on song. There were seconds to go when Wolves were awarded a penalty. Typical, so near and yet so far. The drama wasn't over as Sorensen again pulled off a trade mark penalty save to become the hero, even though he was generally second choice behind Asmir Begovic for Premier League games. We were through and received a kinder home draw against Brighton in the fifth round.

We needed a commanding performance against Brighton and my sons were both excited about Quarter Final possibilities after our run in the previous season that ended at Chelsea. We got our wish and Stoke overpowered Brighton in front of a good crowd of over 21,000. John Carew on loan started the scoring to which Walters and then Shawcross added and it was now all eyes on the draw for the quarter finals.

The result was West Ham at home, about as good as you could hope for. The atmosphere for this one was electric and our wide men Pennant and Etherington were making good runs and delivering tricky crosses. We took the lead through the common routine. Delap's long throw powerfully headed in by Huth which brought the house down. The West Ham equalizer that followed caused controversy as their player Piquionne handled the ball in the break away where he lobbed Sorensen. Early in the second half justice looked to be done when we were awarded a soft penalty. Etherington, an ex Hammer stepped up to take, but it was weakly struck and Rob Green saved. Our golden chance was missed.

With just under thirty minutes remaining we were awarded a free kick just outside the box and straight in front of the goal. We anticipated a Huth thunderbolt or maybe some craft from Pennant, but Danny Higginbotham stepped up to hammer a low shot which flew through the wall and while Rob Green got a good hand to the ball, he couldn't prevent it from creeping over the line. We were

174

ahead again and now we wouldn't let this slip. We held on amid West Ham pressure and huge tension amongst the fans. It was almost unbearable as we all knew that Wembley was beckoning us.

The whistle was pure relief an outflow of emotion, you would have thought we had won the cup, not got to the semi finals. The semi final draw took place immediately after our game so fans watched nervously as the draw took place. The other three teams in the draw were the two Manchester clubs, City and United and Bolton. Obviously we wanted Bolton, Bolton wanted us and the Manchester giants wanted either us or Bolton, but not each other!

The draw was so incredibly important, yes a Wembley appearance was guaranteed, but in all probability a likely defeat by one of these two big guns. Alternatively, we had the prospect of Bolton, a relatively equal Premier League side and one who we could definitely beat and then experience the magic of an FA Cup Final.

The first name out of the hat was Man City (or Reading as their quarter final game kicked off after the draw) and everyone held their breath as the next ball was picked. When the first syllable was Man…, that was enough, we all knew they had been paired together and we would face Bolton. I am sure Bolton fans had the same delirious emotions.

In the run up to the game, the Premier League games were important though seemed like they were just a bit superfluous, like they mattered but didn't really count as the overriding priority became this match at Wembley at 4pm on Sunday 17th April.

I was in Manchester on Thursday 15th on a work Integration project meeting and presentation and I stayed over. This gave me the perfect opportunity to meet an old colleague and friend who, more importantly, was also a Bolton fan. Paul and I met for a beer or three and retired to my hotel for dinner with his partner (now wife and mother of their two children). We had a great time, we always got on well and still do, even though Bolton's fortunes have deteriorated since that Semi Final humiliation. We got through a few bottles and shook hands at the end, it was easy to be humble before the game and Paul was attending with his dad and sons.

I was being picked up in the convoy of lads from Stoke, all the usual crew plus a few extras and we had an appointment at the Green Man, one of Stoke's allocated pubs near Wembley Stadium. We had left early and on this blistering hot day we parked up and began lubricating our vocal chords.

A week or so before the match the business partner in Marketing at the Bank phoned me up asking for a favour. They had multiple requests for the tickets in the Bank's superb box at Wembley for the Man City v United game, but no takers for the glamorous Bolton v Stoke fixture. I told him I would see what I could do. I already had my ticket as did my sons and the box was a large one on the half way line for twelve people. I had been in it once before and was struck by the view immediately you step through the outer door into the box. It was a wall of seats on the other side of the ground, at first view from floor to ceiling spanning the three tiers of red seats, and it was a wonderful sight.

So I took the tickets and I remember when the courier delivered them to my desk at work, having twelve tickets in my hand for the most important Stoke City match I would probably ever attend was a bit frightening. I kept on checking them and just reading them over and over.

I invited some customers who I knew were keen Stoke fans but almost all were already fixed up. So I invited a guy from work, a Stoke fan Ian and his wife, my brother and Tom my youngest wanted to stay in the box too. So Dan, my eldest son and I plotted to start in the box, welcome our guests over a drink, then leave the ground to enter the Stoke seating behind the goal. Then the plan was to leave that area at half time, to arrive back in the box in time for the second half. And then hopefully celebrate back in the box when it was all over. It was all a bit complicated but like the last game at the Vic, I wanted to have it all, every bit of it. I had a couple of tickets left and so invited a guy named Keith. I met Keith after the Quarter Final match against West Ham. He was in the Toby Carvery where I was headed for a meal and a celebratory beer close to my Northampton home. I heard him talking to some of his group about the West Ham match about how great it was and that he was the only Stoke fan from the area in Northampton.

I couldn't resist and went over to him and reassured him he wasn't alone. We got on really well and I sorted him out with two tickets for the box that he thought was magnificent.

So we made our way down from the Green Man and around the outside of this incredible stadium, devouring some food on Wembley Way while we waited for my brother. It was heaven watching the mainly Stoke fans approaching the ground. It was still two hours before kick off and we were excited to get in early. As we approached the Executive entrance under the flyover, there was a mass of security present. As we were about to cross the road and enter I spotted Chris Kamara and made the point of shouting hello, he seemed in good spirits and I took it as a good omen for the day.

Past security, no mean feat, and then through the first set of doors we were met by staff who helped us get through the ticket scanner, that all worked and we were on our way up. The boxes are on Level Three so it was another escalator ride. On Level Three, it was a long way around to the box, all beautifully decorated with wonderful historic photos and pictures of famous Wembley occasions lining the

177

walls. Eventually we found our box and entered. We were the first ones in and had a few moments just family, John, Dan, Tom and I to savour the moment and enjoy a cold Heineken. We opened the sliding doors and went to our seats directly outside the box. It was mesmerizing and the excitement was hard to contain. The others soon joined us and we got ready for the game.

With around twenty minutes to go, it was time for Dan and I to relocate to our seats with our mates and get into the groove behind the goal as we would normally do. When we were leaving the ground to wander to the Stoke fans end, the steward was reluctant to let us out, reminding that tickets couldn't be used for re entry, we got him to open the door and let us out, though he had a look of disbelief on his face. I had spare tickets to get us both back in if all went according to plan during half time, although we would have to be quick as it was quite a trek.

As we settled in and ready for the game, it struck me how enormous this match was. We had listened to the brilliant Pottermouth recording which spoke of Stoke's record at Wembley and about returning to the final in May. It was a battlecry recording that made the hairs on the back of my neck stand up. And now here we were.

I remember that Bolton had the first chance of the game, but it wasn't long before Matty Etherington picked up the ball on the right skipped past a challenge then wrapped his left foot around the ball to send a powerful shot toward goal. It wasn't right in the corner, but before you could blink it was past Jaskelainen in the Bolton goal and in, we were in dreamland. My thoughts returned to the guys in the box and how they must have celebrated, and we were in the middle of one of those too.

Just six minutes later the ball dropped just outside the box, but this time to Robert Huth, our Centre Half, without thinking he volleyed an accurate if not powerful shot curling right towards goal and the scrambling Jaskelainen in goal couldn't get a desperate hand on the ball before it entered the net right in the corner. It was 2 – 0 and it was really on now. We enjoyed that moment which bought us extra space, but there were still nerves, there are always still nerves. On the half hour Kenwynne found himself with space in the box on the left and from a great pass from Pennant he collected the ball, controlled and coolly slotted the ball into the right hand corner for 3 – 0 and complete ecstasy. Now we could relax and enjoy, surely? It had been a truly wonderful first half performance though all the goals had been at the other end. Not complaining, just great to see the net bulge at your end of the ground!

On the whistle Dan and I went downstairs, he decided to stay with the lads in the Stoke end and I had to exit the ground and get back to the Executive entrance again. It was all quite smooth, I ran up the escalator and trotted around the corridor toward the box, and was greeted with hugs and cheers when I went in. Time for a quick visit, a bottle of beer to celebrate and back on it for the second half.

To be honest, while its never done and dusted with Stoke and there was always going to be a reaction from Bolton after the first half, it never really got nervy in the second half. The view from the balcony of the box was fabulous and gave a different perspective of the game than from behind the goal. I didn't sense the usual nerves from the bulk of the fans either as they continued in good voice and celebratory style.

The fourth goal came from pretty much nowhere as John Walters picked up the ball in midfield wide on the left and went on a bit of a run toward goal. He had found a bit of space and while he didn't possess the pace to carry the ball past the defenders, he maneuvered

179

the ball on to his right foot and let fly with perfect accuracy, starting the ball outside the right hand post and curling in. Despite the distance from goal, a good twenty five yards, it beat the keeper again and replays showed just how good a finish it was. At 4 – 0 it was the signal for many Bolton fans to leave and while I wouldn't have done it, you can't totally blame them. The game was up and it was now left for an embarrassing conclusion and in the face of a not very humble Stoke City crowd who were making the most of every moment as the full repertoire of songs rang out around New Wembley.

We celebrated in style on the balcony and it was great to share goals in the first half with Dan and then have the rarest of opportunities to do so again, and again with Tom and my brother John. The fifth goal also arrived as Bolton's heads were well and truly down now and this one could have been the icing to top all icings as Wilko had got forward and from an angle prodded the ball toward goal, it was deflected out but only to John Walters who finished the job and we were record winners in the Semi Final.

The sun kept shining, we were 5 – 0 up and the fridge was still half full of ice cold Heineken. After enjoying the player celebrations on the final whistle and roundly clapped them off the field, I heard my name being called, it was from the Club Wembley seats directly below us where Mike (the Mack) reached up to shake hands with me. This was Mike who endured the play off semi final heartache at Gillingham and who celebrated wildly with me at Charlton as Stefan Thordarson scored that thirty yard howitzer. Now he was here also witnessing history and like me, I think he deserved every minute of the pleasure it generated.

Eventually it was time to leave the stadium and we made our way back up to the Green Man pub to meet the lads, everyone was just so incredibly pleased and proud of our performance and our only problem was that Ade's car battery was flat. We soon enlisted the help of someone with jump leads and we and the other drivers in our convoy started the journey home.

Tickets for the final were a bit harder to come by but as usual, from our various sources as season ticket holders and other contacts and connections with the club, we sourced the full requirement for the final.

Man City were going to be very tough opponents, with Tevez, Yaya Toure, Balotelli and David Silva in their ranks but we were playing well and despite some injuries to key players we still believed.

For me this was fate, a thirty five year journey which started against Man City at home in the FA Cup to now repeat that fixture on Wembley's hallowed turf, and at a stadium, be it Old or New Wembley where we had won on all our previous four visits. The ticket situation meant there was a spare and I snapped it up. I wanted to invite John, he was responsible for me seeing my first game and was with me at the semi final where we demolished Bolton. If this was meant to be, then John should be there to see it. He accepted it gladly as an early birthday present.

The travel arrangements for this one were slightly different as the Green Man was allocated to Man City for the final so we took a different route and found a good space in JJMoons pub, full of Stokies near Kingsbury station where we had parked up. Again I was picked up from home being conveniently (for me) on the way. I was nervous and I had texted Ade the night before about my nerves, he abruptly put me straight saying that we will play well and we will win. I believed him, but still didn't sleep too well.

We began with breakfast at Toddington services, where we bought our Cup Final Programmes (which was great so we could leave these in the car and save them from being all creased and folded up). Then after a team photo in the car at Kingsbury we got to the pub early. Some of the younger crew wanted food so I took them including my two sons over to Nandos which passed the time and helped settle the nerves. It didn't feel like we were really going to the cup final. That it would be us watching our team playing rather than settling in front of the TV to watch the brass band marching, the fans wandering up Wembley way and Abide With Me and the National Anthem ringing out.

At Wembley we met my brother again, and this time as we were about to enter we saw Garth Crooks, so a quick hello and a bit less of a smile than Kammy had offered at the semi final. We were soon heading for the turnstiles. John had turned up in a bright yellow tee shirt, so I got the beers in and sent my lads to get him a scarf from the stall inside the ground. That was much better and he still proudly displays the scarf and the Cup Final ticket at his home in Dorchester.

As for the game, well the readers of this book will either have been there, seen the TV footage or heard the reports, so I am only reporting personal highlights for me. The injuries we had sustained were definitely affecting us and while Huth and Etherington started, they were clearly struggling.

My highlights of the day are the amazing Stoke supporters who gave unstinting vocal support and even stayed to the bitter end as Man City collected the trophy, rather than in most cases leaving to avoid seeing the cup presented. TV pundits and Man City fans alike applauded this which was unusual. Also the pre match ritual of singing Abide With Me and the National Anthem which brought a tear to my eye.

182

As for the game, it was great that Sorensen was rewarded again by starting in goal, and he lived up to that decision with some fine saves including a stunning tip over that was heading for the top corner from Balotelli. We made it to half time at 0 – 0 which was a relief as we hadn't created anything threatening.

In the second half, before the Man City goal and winner from Yaya Toure, we had the one moment that could of changed everything. A long ball found Kenwynne in space and he ran into the box for a one on one with Joe Hart. Kenny tried to slip the ball under Hart whose left leg just caught the ball and deflected it away. Many will say great save, I thought he got lucky.

The goal came and we understandably became desperate and threw on Carew who was still on loan with us. We had a half chance right at the death but it came to nothing and we did what Stoke do best, lost narrowly in a hard fought contest after putting up a spirited struggle. That's actually a bit unfair on the lads, we really gave our all with injured players and against a team with the deepest pockets in the world. We were rightfully proud of our team and we had earned a place in the Europa League, where we entered in the third qualifying round, so we would be able to watch our side pit ourselves against European opposition as well as the Premier League giants. For all this we thank Tony Pulis and even if our feelings for him differ between supporters, no one can ever take away what he helped us to achieve in this historic season.

183

CHAPTER TWENTYONE
Europe

Being back working with my previous boss to get the portfolio of good Real Estate loans onto the Mid Markets balance sheet gave me a new lease of life at the Bank. I was working with people who I trusted and who were highly commercial, which meant we could get things done.

The call inviting me to do this work came while I was on holiday at my Brother's house in Dorchester. I was on Weymouth beach with my sons having a game of footie on a lovely sunny day. In that same week on 28th July, just a day before my youngest son Tom's eleventh birthday, we also played our first away trip in Europe since 1974 against Ajax (ignoring the Anglo Italian Cup we appeared in during the 1993 and 1994 seasons).

The draw for the third qualifying round included seventy teams and we were about to realise what a commitment it was to take a competitive part in the Europa League. We could have drawn the likes of Sligo Rovers, or Club Brugge for example which would have been wonderful trips; Bruges is one of my favourite Cities in the world, but we ended up against Hajduk Split. They were an intimidating opponent who were used to European football and had won championships in the old Yugoslavia as well as five consecutive Yugoslav Cups, they have been in the quarterfinals of the European Cup and a UEFA and Cup Winners Cup semi finals.

So the draw wasn't kind to us. Our first game was at home and a large crowd of 26,322 saw the game. Among that number were many Croatians who set off flares and made a real spectacle. Luckily for us we scored an early settling goal through a John Walters header. We remained on top but with few clear cut chances and at the end a win and a clean sheet was how we commenced our campaign. We all hoped that we could continue the journey. Quite a few of the lads went to the away leg where the crowd was an even bigger 29,548. They recall an intimidating arena and well rehearsed policing that kept everything in order. I regret not getting to this one, and for all I knew it might have been our only opportunity. The boys and I managed to get a crackly stream while we were on holiday in Dorchester with my Brother and we seemed to be in reasonable control without too many scares until Ryan Shotton scored a very late winner to seal the match and the tie. We were going through.

Our reward for overcoming Hajduk Split was another Play Off Round, where victory again would mean access to the Europa League proper. All eyes on the draw again and this time while we could have had a more glamorous tie, we were paired against FC Thun, a small Swiss club set in the foothills of the Jungfrau, the highest mountain in the Alps. A simply stunning location.

I was in the process of being offered an opportunity to continue my stay at Lloyds and couldn't get to the away leg. I looked into it and it seemed a tricky journey. My friend Owen went on the official coach which he says was a memorable if very long journey and he was grateful for the locals in Thun for buying some beer for the Stoke fans, as general cost of living and alcohol in particular is extremely expensive. I remember some footage of a couple of Stoke fans jumping off a bridge in the town into a very inviting looking river which was such a beautiful blue/green colour. I also know that the temperature of that water, running straight off the Alps would have been absolutely freezing.

This time it was the away leg first and our hopes were high for the match, enhanced by a goal from Danny Pugh after nineteen minutes to give us the advantage which is how the game ended. Three games played and three wins with three clean sheets, amazing. At home there was again a very good crowd though not so many away fans this time. We exploited our aerial advantage perfectly and between Upson and Kenny, with a Whelan shot in between, we blew them away and while they scored a late consolation, that's all it was and we were through, 5 – 1 on aggregate this time.

I was on holiday with my wife a couple of years ago in Interlaken and for this journey we flew to Zurich and took the most scenic rail journey ever to the beautiful town of Interlaken also close to the highest peaks in the Alps. Enroute the second last stop was Thun and I saw the floodlights from the train. If I had done my research properly I think I could have made the journey as it was actually fairly straightforward. Oh well, next time!

After four games we now got to compete in the Group stage in a league with three other teams with the top two going through to the Round of Thirty Two teams. It was then a pure knockout competition.

The draw for the Group stage brought more excitement and while some sides were seeded, there was a massive range of clubs we could thoroughly enjoy being drawn against and to have some European adventures.

We were joined in the Group stages by Spurs, who drew PAOK (Greece), Rubin Kazan (Russia) and Shamrock Rovers. And also by Birmingham City who got through by amazingly beating Arsenal in the League Cup Final (and then getting relegated in the same season). They had the luxury of Club Brugge, Braga (Portugal) and Maribor. Other UK teams were Celtic, who drew a tricky group with Atletico Madrid, Udinese and Rennes. Fulham drew FC Twente (Holland) Wisla Krakow (Poland) and Odense (Denmark).

So who would we get? Well we drew Maccabi Tel Aviv (I didn't know Israeli teams were involved in the Europa League and not your everyday nip across the channel for an away trip). Next was Dynamo Kiev, Ukrainian giants. Lastly Besiktas, Turkey, thanks a lot, not a sniff of France, Belgium or Germany. This was probably the hardest group in the competition.

Our first task was away at Dynamo Kiev and while the Kiev team were not the legend that previous sides had been, this was still a real challenge. We kept it tight and had four players yellow carded, including centre halves Huth, Shawcross and Upson. We weathered the storm and scored a good goal in the second half through Cameron Jerome and held on to this until the very last minute when we conceded. Still a great opening result away in this tough league.

Next up was Besiktas, Turkish European stalwarts. A large crowd at home for this one with Peter Crouch, newly signed from Spurs in our ranks and who had scored his first goal for Stoke at the weekend against Man United. Crouchy did it again with an equalizing header just a minute after they had taken the lead. It was just as well as Besiktas were formidable opponents and could easily have scored a second but for the post. We dug in and won a penalty just before half time. John Walters scored powerfully to give us the lead. This was how it stayed and three valuable points were earned to keep us in a good position in our mini league.

Our next two games were against the weakest side in the league, Maccabi Tel Aviv. I looked at flights to Tel Aviv, it was an expensive option and I just couldn't justify it at the time. The home game was first and first half goals from Kenny, Jerome and Shotton again effectively killed the game, though Jerome being sent off didn't help and might have cost us valuable goal difference. But they had a player sent off in the second half as their player Ziv angrily kicked his boot (that had came off in a challenge) at the linesman which hit him square on. Very funny.

We dominated in the away leg and controlled the game in the rain in Tel Aviv where first Whitehead and then Peter Crouch scored to put two up. Again we conceded a very late consolation goal (three times now) but three more points and we were top of our league.

The final two group games would decide our qualification and they were tough matches against first Dynamo Kiev at home and then Besiktas away.

The Kiev game was a thriller in which they dominated the first half and took the lead after seven minutes. It could have been worse as Shevchenko missed a good chance. We upped the intensity in the second half and got a deserved equalizer in the 80th minute after a towering header by Kenwynne. This is how I choose to remember Kenwynne, not the way many fans portray him and on this day he secured the goal, the draw and the point that meant we had already qualified before taking on Besiktas on 14th December.

I didn't travel for the Besiktas game and watched a lively affair on TV. We took the lead through Fuller with a vicious deflected shot and so nearly doubled that lead shortly afterwards after the ball rebounded off the bar. I felt Ricky was fouled when trying to reach the rebound. Besiktas then dominated and not even a string of fine saves from Begovic could deny them. It was a weakened Stoke side that day as we had already qualified and in the end a 3 – 1 loss, our first in the competition, gave Besiktas the points and top place in the group. We were second which gave us a tougher draw. But we were through!

At the end of the Group stage we were the only UK team who made it through to the last 32 and now all eyes were on that draw. I had my eyes on Ajax and Steve said a sunny Valencia trip was his preference. It ended up being Valencia and this meant two very tasty ties, the first at the Brit followed by the away leg at the Mestella Stadium in Valencia. We were all eagerly anticipating both occasions. We were at home first and a nearly full house with the exception of some empty seats in the away fans area. We settled down for what we hoped would be another good home result and had been unbeaten in both the qualifying ties and the Group stage at home.

Valencia were a different proposition to the others and that was obvious right from the start. They have a rich European track record and history and probably saw us as we had seen some of the teams in our earlier matches. Despite early pressure our goal never came and they scored a cracker from out of the blue with a scorching shot from Mehmet Topal. The game ended 1 – 0 to Valencia and while this wasn't the score line we wanted, we were still in the tie and had already made plans and booked our journey to sunny Spain.

We flew as a group from Luton and headed for Madrid, then it was a long road trip to Valencia. It was an early start from Luton and everyone was in good spirits as we took over the back few rows on the Easyjet flight. I prepared a quiz to keep the lads occupied and even those who dosed off weren't really relaxing as the anticipation grew and grew. From Madrid we hired a couple of cars and packed ourselves in for the long but scenic journey on a warm sunny afternoon. After stopping for some lunch at some services we drifted into town and made ourselves at home at our hotel in the centre.

A quick change and we were in the Finnegans Irish pub, near the Cathedral where many Stoke fans had already congregated. The songs were ringing out and it just felt like everyone was going to make the most of this trip and a rare opportunity to compete on foreign soil. We all enjoyed a large Paella before continuing the drinks and banter at the bar adjoined to our hotel which also contained many Stoke fans, but less rowdy and none of the plastic glasses nonsense. We stayed there till well after midnight and planned our formations with empty glasses and bottles on the table while the beer flowed.

Some of the older guys, me included drifted upstairs to our rooms leaving a few youngsters behind, Rosco, Joe and Emma. I was sharing with Steve Fryer who has wicked sense of humour and a very dirty laugh. He had retired to bed a little before me and when I got to the room I had a change of heart, and from starting to undress, decided that it was a one off and I would return to see it through with the youngsters. Steve was a bit confused by this as I disappeared again and carried on where I had left off with a round of drinks for the lads (Emma knows that includes her, she is one of the boys really and can shift a few pints).

I am not sure what time we packed in, there were still Stoke fans in the bar but it was quieter now and we were well oiled. Joe and Rosco were sharing and had a bit of an incident in their room, enough said. Emma just had a sore head in the morning.

When morning came the lads all went off for breakfast and were heading down to the beach. I was in no fit state to join and needed the extra hour or so to come around gently. A small breakfast and taxi ride took me to the beach at around midday and the lads were all set up for a game of footy on the beach opposite the very plush looking hotel where we learnt the players were staying.

We had a good game and while playing football wasn't a regular past time for me I did have a couple of good moments. I especially remember getting a good shot away through the legs of the blocker, it was heading for the corner and I was starting to celebrate. In goal was Max, Ade's son and a very tall lad, he arrived from nowhere to get a hand on my shot and turned it around the post. I never scored many and he denied me a famous one on Valencia beach for which I continue to remind him. On our side was Joe. Joe was a nasty tackler and the was an audible gasp when he lunged a challenge at his sister Emma in the midfield. We didn't really want to be spending the day in A&E and luckily it ended without broken bones, although she gave him one hell of a clout afterwards.

It was hot and we packed up shortly afterwards before any major injuries were sustained. At the hotel grounds fence we saw some of the players and got a wave from our heroes. This is when we learned that Pulis had left some important players behind, including Crouchy. I know why he did it, he was concerned that we could still be relegated and wanted to prioritize the league. Being fair to him we won our next two home games against Swansea and Norwich which pretty much did the job, but we did feel a bit let down that, with such an invasion of Stoke fans, we wouldn't see our best eleven trying to claw back the deficit and maybe even go on to win in Valencia.

After just a quick break for a drink some of the lads wanted to go to the ground and visit the club shop for some souvenirs. And that's where the Spanish language incident occurred. We had hailed a cab and were piling in. One of the lads, Steve started to give instructions to the driver when Simon (T4) stepped in, like Roger Moore in The Man with the Golden Gun, arms out holding us back and saying "Leave this to me, I'm the Spanish speaker". So we gave him his moment. I was in the car by this time when Simon cleared his throat and said, "Ola" (good start), followed by "El Club Shop". The driver knew what we wanted and while T4 was quite pleased with his efforts, we were absolutely doubled up pissing ourselves. He had employed his entire Spanish vocabulary!

The Club Shop was unsurprisingly at the Ground and the guys headed in. I took in the stadium views with a hundred or so other

Stokies in bright sunshine looking up at the steep upper tiered terrace of the ground which would house many Stoke fans and particularly those who had obtained tickets through our Club. It was quite a sight, old fashioned and imposing. I shared a beer with a few Stoke fans and then we were all back to the hotel for final preparations.

Final preparations involved getting my England/Stoke flag in a good position on the hotel roof on the twelfth floor and visible from the narrow park area and bars opposite where the guys had settled. I found a good spot on the next to top floor where I could secure the flag, it still simply displayed DAN and TOM in the top quadrants and SCFC in the bottom left. The bottom right quarter having been mutilated in Germany prior to the World Cup match against Trinidad & Tobago.

After a beer or two surveying the handy work I made one last visit to the hotel and was met by a receptionist who told me I had to move the flag. Clearly it was even more visible than I had intended.

I took the lift to the twelfth floor and took it down, but then noticed an even more prominent spot on the actual roof of the hotel which I managed to reach by some outside stairs that were quite clearly not for public use. They had told me to move the flag, and so I did. Up one floor to the very roof and we had a good view of the flag as we wandered toward the ground with an army of Stoke fans lining the entire route.

That was the last time I ever saw the flag. It had been to Portugal for the Euros, to Germany for the World Cup and also to Brisbane where I proudly displayed it as England began their disastrous Ashes campaign in 2006.

At the ground we found a good spot on the bottom tier of the end of the ground where Stoke fans were everywhere and notably in that high area of terracing which was now above us. The game didn't work out for us though we had two glorious chances that both fell to Kenny. The first was a clear chance on goal in the box against the keeper and then an even better headed opportunity. He fluffed his lines on both occasions and after Valencia scored that was it.

We battled manfully, with many lads playing who hadn't had a game for some time and we looked back wondering what might have been.

The following day we were on a tight timescale to catch our plane home from Madrid. Simon Travis was driving and we needed to take a particular exit from the complicated ring road to reach Terminal Four. First attempt was a failure and unbeknown to us this meant a several mile detour and loss of time we barely had left to check in. Second attempt, and all the other four passengers were now also on the case to make sure there was no slip up. Bugger me he went straight past it again and now we were in trouble. To make things worse we got cut up and Simon went bananas and chased the guy for a mile or two shouting expletives. We were more concerned with executing the manoeuvre to take the correct exit, which if we missed again would mean missing our flight. We got there, it was tight and we were at Terminal Four. Simon is now and forever known as T4.

Our adventure was over. We had played twelve games in this campaign. Had we progressed to the final this would have meant a further seven games which totals half a full season in the Premier League. I can understand the mixed reception that qualifying for the Europa League generates, it really does interfere with the domestic campaign but for me, the opportunity to watch Stoke City in Europe overwhelms all of the negativity that's displayed by some clubs about the tournament.

193

Maybe they shouldn't even compete in it if its just too much trouble and convey the place to a club who can appreciate the opportunity. Spurs are one of the worst at this and I know many Arsenal fans say the day after Wednesday is Spursday when their rivals take part in their usual European competition.

As for the domestic league and cup competitions in a season dominated by European adventures, we started the league steadily two draws and two wins. First the inevitable win against West Brom and then Liverpool both at home. Then we had a bad run containing six defeats in eight games including some nasty results on Sundays immediately following Europa League fixtures. Swansea and Bolton were the beneficiaries, in Bolton's case reversing the Wembley Semi Final score with their own 5 – 0 victory (it wasn't enough for them to stay up however and we inflicted the final blow equalizing at home through a John Walters penalty to consign them to the Championship).

Then, as if a switch flicked again, we enjoyed some stunning wins away at Everton; Huth scoring the winner, and also at Wolves. This combined with home victories over Blackburn and Spurs meant we were back on track.

Our home defeat (against the run of play) against West Brom on 21st January 2012 was the first reverse against them, home and away, in almost a decade, the last one being the 1 – 0 defeat in September 2003 at the Hawthorns. After three more defeats in a row Tony Pulis was prompted to take a weakened squad to Valencia. He was protecting the squad ahead of the next two games at home against Swansea and Norwich.

We won both in solid fashion, 2 – 0 and 1 – 0 respectively which eased any thoughts of being dragged into the relegation mix.

Against Man City at home a day before my 51st birthday, Crouchy gave us something special to cheer as he controlled a header from Jermaine Pennant on his chest before sending a powerful volley toward the top corner from outside the corner of their box leaving Joe Hart completely stranded. How we missed that talent away at Valencia!

A finish in 14th was a little off the pace of the previous two years, but perfectly safe and we had had our fun!

The FA Cup gave us another good run, ended at Liverpool in the Quarter Finals (again) after Crouchy had equalized and given us great hope of a first win at Anfield since 1959. The Scousers also knocked us out of the League Cup after Kenny had given us the lead with a trademark header.

The summer brought more change at work as I narrowly missed out on the permanent MD role but stayed on in an interim role in this position while the successful candidate, Marty Green, arrived from Melbourne, Australia. Marty's move to the UK and the work permit was complicated to resolve and gave me the chance to extend my stay where the team had settled down after all the earlier change. We were now able to spend time more productively with customer related activity rather than looking over our shoulder for the next restructure, which had become business as usual at the bank.

CHAPTER TWENTY TWO
More Premier League Years and
Pulis hands over to Hughes

When Marty arrived from Melbourne to head up the team that I had been in charge of, things could have gone one of two ways. Either he wouldn't want me around and I would then exit the bank, or, as actually happened we got on like a house on fire and he felt that I knew so much about the business and the people that I was almost indispensible.

This was a bit double edged. I was pleased to be needed and retained in a senior leadership role, but on the other hand I had reconciled myself to leaving and was looking forward to being liberated. However, I was enjoying working with Marty so stayed put and did my best to help him navigate within the bank, which was a tricky operation. As a business we had conflicting objectives. We were directed to work within a strict lending cap for the Real Estate sector at the same time as our Chief Executive ordered his customer facing business to increase lending to SME (Small & Medium sized Enterprises). Our customers fell directly into that category.

The reason for such a focus on lending were the promises made to the Government, its major shareholder. Lloyds had undertaken to keep on lending, under the banner of "Helping Britain Prosper".

The problem was that while the recession was over, businesses were not confident enough to invest in capital expenditure projects and so general trading enterprises across the UK were not looking to borrow large sums of money. In the Real Estate sector however, there was demand by investors who saw an opportunity to gain advantage from Property Markets at a relative low point.

In the short term, while there was lots of talk about risk etc the priority of growing the balance sheet won hands down and we were instructed to lend, lend, lend. Updates were required weekly to the Chief Executive. The lending we did was "sticky lending" in that when loans were drawn, they stuck on the balance sheet for their full term (typically 3 to 5 years). In other parts of the bank teams were only doing overdrafts and short term facilities, but as these revolved it didn't grow the balance sheet. In Real Estate, we could directly grow the balance sheet and having been seen for years by the bank as the rotten apple in the barrel, we were now its potential saviour.

Ultimately Marty's boss paid the price because the lending numbers weren't growing fast enough and we were left in the heavy gaze of the bank's Chief Executive Antionio Horta Osorio. It was as though all that mattered was the growth in lending that had been promised.

The 2012/13 football season started meekly. We didn't know at that point that it would be Tony Pulis's last season in charge at the club. The opener away at Reading on a blistering hot day saw us draw 1 – 1 and new signing Michael Kightly scored to put us ahead. We caved in at the death and conceded a penalty which was converted. Then after a succession of draws, the discontent which had been building, seemed to grow arms and legs and the undercurrent of unrest surfaced amongst the fans.

We still had our moments and although the scores were becoming quite binary again, we secured enough wins to keep out of trouble in the league. This never really satisfied fans and away from home it was turgid. The high spot was the home win against Liverpool on Boxing Day where we won despite going behind in the first few

197

minutes as a clumsy penalty was given away and dispatched by Steven Gerrard. John Walters and Kenwynne Jones provided the goals to send us away happy and then just three days later we enjoyed a thriller against Southampton where we drew 3 – 3 thanks to a late cracker by Cameron Jerome from thirty yards in the last minute of injury time. Dan, Tom and I were on the stairs ready to leave on the final whistle when he scored and the celebrations on the stairs of the Boothen End reminded me of the old times.

We then lost ten of the next thirteen games and were in trouble again. We even lost at home to relegation threatened Aston Villa and the discontent was more evident than ever.

A couple of good wins against fellow strugglers QPR and Norwich eased the tension.

Our last home game was against Spurs and arrangements were in place to mark the 150th anniversary of the club, the second longest established football club on the planet since 1863.

It was a rainy dreary day in Stoke and while many heroes from the past were paraded around the ground to fans, it felt like there was something missing. The game also didn't live up to expectations. We took an early lead through a rare Steven Nzonzi header, Charlie Adam got himself sent off needlessly and we eventually crumbled to a 2 – 1 defeat.

That left our last game of the season at Southampton and we had arranged an overnight stay for all the usual crowd on the night before. There was a good away following and a fairly boisterous atmosphere fuelled by a dozen or so Saints fans in ill fitting Black Tie attire winding us up throughout the first half. The celebrations started when Peter Crouch deftly glanced a header in at our end. It didn't last and we drew 1 – 1 with Michael Owen coming on in his final ever match. He had a chance to mark it with a goal, but the touch he displayed for much of his career had deserted him.

We all knew that this would be Michael's last game and we gave him a great send off for which he was very appreciative. What we didn't know was that it would be Tony's last game as well. Anyway we left relatively contented for the journey home.

Back at the Bank, I was asked to assume responsibility for the Social Housing team (again) and lead the very important value creation work through that team. The Social Housing team had over £10 billion of debt exposure to Housing Associations. Most loans were on very long term arrangements that had become loss making to the Bank as their cost of funds had risen steeply during the Financial Crisis. The Bank had chosen the greedy option to maximize profitability and fund these long term loans through short term funding lines such as the Interbank Market and through customer deposits. This worked well until the music stopped.

Our job was to manage the Bank debt down or restructure and re-price it to make it less loss making and eventually profitable again. The team were doing a brilliant job using the Capital Markets through Bond Issuance and Private Placements (basically introducing external investors to supply the long term debt instead of the Bank).

After the merger, Lloyds became the market leader overnight as both HBoS and Lloyds had large lending commitments to the sector. We did some of the most important deals within the Bank during the next 18 months. It wasn't seen as a particularly glamorous but the impact of the team's results were making a significant impact on the profitability of the business.

While running this team I had the enjoyable opportunity to work with Tony Oakley, a passionate West Ham fan and season ticket holder. Tony and I became and remain close friends and his company and our occasional laughter and a glass of Peroni helped us both through a tricky period of change at Lloyds. Tony's mobile number comes up on my phone as Tony Peroni and we will share a few more of those before we are done.

2013/14 Season

Exit Tony Pulis and enter Mark Hughes, I discuss this in my chapter on Managers so I will get straight to the action. Hughes brought in Marco Arnautovic for what now seems a bargain £2m and Erik Pieters also joined at Left Back. The feeling was that we were light up front although Peter Crouch will always knock a few in and John Walters keeps on proving his usefulness.

Kenwynne however had lost his mojo, or the entire plot some would say and was little help to the goals scored statistics. He proved this in the last minute of our opener, a tricky game at Anfield when we started promisingly with Huth hitting the bar with a powerful volley. We went behind and in chasing the game were leaving ourselves quite open, but in the last minute we won a penalty for handball. I called it as soon as I saw the action and while the decision surprised quite a few, this was our chance. Walters stepped up and Mignolet saved low to his right, Mignolet is not a great keeper, but his specialty are penalty saves. The rebound was a yard out and Kenwynne was first to the ball, surely he would bury it and deliver the equalizer, but a half hearted shot was also saved when he should have given the keeper no chance. It felt like we were robbed, but in truth we robbed ourselves.

We won at home to Palace the following week and followed that up with an excellent Pennant free-kick at West Ham in a game we dominated. A home draw against Man City came next and we looked well placed. Then we lost four of the next five, albeit one was at Arsenal where I celebrated Cameron's well taken goal much to the annoyance of the Arsenal fans around me. I had been invited to the game and had promised to behave. At Old Trafford, we showed courage and talent as first Crouch and then a wonderful free-kick by Arnie gave us the lead twice. Arnie has taken many free-kicks since, not one has troubled the keeper.

Next was a lucky draw at home to Southampton, where Begovic, our keeper scored from his own box as the wind caught his huge goal kick. Then at Swansea, a very late penalty in the ninety fifth minute, coolly slotted home by Charlie Adam, gave us a draw. We had been 2 – 0 up at Swansea, but also found ourselves 3 – 2 behind so the penalty was a welcome relief.

After a home win against Sunderland, Dan and I took advantage of the coach travel to go to Everton, one of the few grounds I had never visited. It was a lovely sunny day and we have had some great results at Everton. Not on this day where we lost 4 – 0.

We held it together and won at home against Chelsea with Assaidi cutting in and from well outside the box sending an unstoppable and swerving shot into the top corner in the final minute. Even Jose congratulated Assaidi for that one.

It was an up and down season and my highlight of the New Year was the home win against Man Utd. We had waited for that and Charlie's fabulous strike gave us the 2 – 1 lead we would defend with our lives.

March was excellent for us with four wins and a draw including the demolition at Aston Villa 4 – 1 which gave us a real glimpse of what we might be capable of. With the smiling Odemwingie now in the squad, swapped for the toothless Kenwynne Jones, we looked more active and potent.

We dismantled Fulham at home, then on the final day won with a late goal from Charlie Adam at West Brom (Déjà vu?) I would loved to have attended but couldn't get a hand on a ticket.

We had rediscovered our away form and tickets for away games were now much more sought after. This demonstrated the progress from the Pulis years of watching through gritted teeth and fearing the inevitable, knowing that to concede generally meant the end of the game.

In the cups we reached the League Cup quarter final where Man Utd beat us in the wind and hail at the Britannia. Not our best performance. In the FA Cup we drew Chelsea in the 4th Round and were dispatched 1 – 0, in a brave but never very likely to get a result, type of performance.

Back to the league, we had finished 9th, our best ever Premier League finish with a record fifty points. It didn't really feel like a top half and fifty points type of season, but it's there for all to see. I am sure Mark Hughes pointed this out at his year end performance review.

Back at Lloyds, Marty was trying desperately hard to get a fair hearing for the Real Estate team and made several high level presentations to very senior guys and to the Risk team. The Risk team or teams now, had acquired even more sway as the economy wasn't picking up as positively as it first appeared and the potential consequences of another downturn on the Real Estate markets were giving them the jitters.

I didn't and still don't buy the level of scaremongering coming from the Credit and Risk areas. Our credit policy meant our lending had been very prudent, on good established assets and where there would need to be a seismic shift to endanger any of the banks money.

2014/15 Season

I liked the new signings, Bojan, who I'd never heard of arrived from Barcelona and Mame Diouf who we had been after for a while up front, Sidwell and wingers Moses and Assaidi also arrived. Looking good!

The loss at home to Villa was a real set back and added to that a scrambled point at Hull, with thanks to Ryan for his late equalizer. Then amazingly we won at Man City with Diouf on the score sheet, thanks Joe Hart for being a useless keeper, either of my sons would have kept that Diouf effort out.

Both Leicester and Burnley beat us at home. It was very quiet in the car on the trips home from these games. Our form was flattering to deceive. We won at Spurs, then lost 2 – 1 at home to Burnley. At Man Utd we somehow also lost 2 – 1. Nzonzi scored a wicked goal with a bullet shot to equalize and even though they took the lead again (with an offside goal) there was the most amazing scramble just a yard or two out where both Arnie and Diouf smacked shots against De Gea. Dan and I who had taken the coach from the Brit for the second time just couldn't believe we hadn't got at least a draw out of that game.

In our next ten games, we won five, drew three and lost just two. The home game against Arsenal may not look as though we took them apart with a 3 – 2 score line, but we did. At 3 – 0 up we had a fourth disallowed through Bojan and I think it could have been a real rout. Maybe we saved it for Liverpool and Steven Gerrard's last game!

So with the team on good form only losing two out of ten, I took Marty to the Emirates telling him about our passionate support and our expansive play. We got mullered 3 – 0. Marty, it transpires has family connections from Stoke on Trent and his grandfather had a connection with the club. He didn't immediately let on when we met that he had a soft spot for Stoke City, but its an ingredient that certainly helped us bond. It was great to have an Australian Stoke City fan on board, especially my boss. So when I got some stick from some of the guys at work after or before a game, he often stepped in to give his backing. I didn't need it but it was very amusing. Anyway I took him to Arsenal and we were well beaten. The away fans were also quite subdued and uncharacteristically, sat for most of the game.

We perked up and won at Leicester through Bojan with a great turn and goal from the edge of the box and then John Walters got a hat trick against QPR to give us a resounding home win. I also liked Crouchy's late looping header to equalize against Newcastle away, which we just about deserved.

By this time I was working back in Birmingham where I had been asked to fill in for a colleague and friend, Ian Martin who had decided to leave the Bank. This meant I left Social Housing behind in the safe hands of Tony Oakley. Soon after I assumed responsibility for all of the regional Real Estate offices outside of London. I was invited as head of the team to the Villa away game by a local law firm and had a bet on the full time score at good odds. I went with 2 – 1 and was on best behaviour in the box which was a long way away from our noisy away support in the ground and near the Holte End. Diouf equalized with a very good header just before half time and then in injury time Moses danced through the Villa defence and went down. Penalty given and this was squeaky bum time. Moses placed the ball and only seemed to be a yard or so away from the spot. He nonchalantly stepped up and rolled the ball into the corner of the net with the keeper stranded in the opposite corner. It was the calmest penalty I have ever seen. We won the game and I won my bet.

We lost at West Brom, that's not so strange now that Tony is their manager, whereas previously it was almost unheard of.

Our last three games started with a home game against Spurs where we ran out comfortable 3 – 0 winners. That doesn't happen often and since then they have cut us to ribbons home and away.

Next was Burnley away where we earned a stubborn draw. And our final game was eagerly awaited against Liverpool where Steven Gerrard would play his last game for the club. Tickets were changing hands for silly money and Liverpool fans especially were seeking ways to get into the ground.

Dan, Tom and I were staying over and were making the most of the day and night. A sunny day, already a fifty one point record haul and 9th place guaranteed and that's even before kick off. This proved to be a memorable game and Diouf scored the opener after twenty two minutes after Mignolet could only parry Adam's shot. The same striker tried his luck just four minutes later and this time his shot flew in past a helpless Mignolet to make in 2 - 0. The Brit was rocking and the pressure was unrelenting. Walters made the most from a mix up in the box again involving Mignolet and scored. We were then 3 – 0 up after just thirty minutes and we weren't done. Charlie Adam collected the ball in their half and went on a run shooting low and hard from well outside the box, it was perfectly placed and even a scrambling Mignolet couldn't keep it out, 4 – 0 and we were in heaven. I saw many fans heading down to get in the bar queue for a celebratory beer, but our group stayed put, we knew this was special and we weren't going to miss a single moment.

On the stroke of half time Steven Nzonzi waltzed through the midfield, he could be incredibly graceful on the ball and was a talent that we didn't fully appreciate enough at Stoke. Since he left us in the close season for £8m to Seville, we have never found a complete replacement. Anyway on this day he carried the ball toward the box before he checked and then elegantly curled a beauty into the top corner to make it 5 – 0.

This was the best half time interval I had ever experienced, with the possible exception of the Wembley FA Cup Semi Final.

Call me greedy, but I wanted more, I wanted to erase the 8 – 0 result in the League Cup all those years before and while I didn't begrudge Gerrard his goal which he created and took well, I wanted the game to be remembered for the battering we gave them. So when Crouchy came on and promptly headed in number six, the balance was restored and though it was our last goal on the day that had taken us to 54 points, a Premier League record for the club and 9th place again, we all felt that we might be on the verge of something quite special. It had been over 50 years since Liverpool had conceded six goals.

In the cups we let ourselves down a bit and Dan and I had travelled to Rochdale to watch us play so well and win comfortably 4 – 1. Bojan scored the special first goal on the night. He suffered a long term injury shortly afterwards in the match that kept him out for the rest of the season. This was a real blow and he never returned quite the same player. A large group of us travelled to Blackburn on Valentines Day to hopefully watch us progress to the Quarter Finals, however despite a massive away following and an early lead courtesy of Peter Crouch, we crumbled to a sad 4 – 1 defeat against this lower league opposition.

In the League Cup we also looked promising. After a good away win at Sunderland where Marc Muniesa scored twice in a 2 – 1 win we were at home to Southampton next. Tom, Dan and I had travelled up to Stoke in half term and were staying over to enjoy the occasion and in the likely event there was extra time and a late finish.

The Saints took the lead through an exquisite strike by Pelle, with a perfect curler and things got worse when Shane Long doubled their lead on the half hour, both at our end. The half time team talk must have been good as we came our all guns blazing and Nzonzi rampaged through the midfield and fired a long distance effort into the corner to make it 2 - 1. Then the noise levels increased further as lots of pressure from corners resulted in Diouf heading home from a flick to equalize.

We were now the better team and looked the likelier winners. However the task was made much harder when Crouch was dismissed with just a couple of minutes remaining for a second bookable offence and we were facing the prospect of extra time with ten men. Extra time was not needed in the end as almost instantly after the sending off, Pelle scored their winner in the 89th minute and we had contrived to get knocked out after a storming comeback.

At work, I was travelling between Birmingham, Manchester, Leeds, Edinburgh and Bristol to manage various teams located in these regions. I was spending a couple or three nights away from home each week. It was the archetypal spinning plates routine and the geography complicated that. The Bank had also bound itself up with layers of compliance and regulation and I was being cut no slack in recognition of these complex regional responsibilities. In short it was becoming a chore.

I enjoyed working with my colleagues across the UK and many really interesting customers, however, the micro management we were subjected to was driving me mad. Relentless mandatory training, activity logs and tracking of customer and professionals meetings, all the associated work of ten direct reports, monthly 121s and performance meetings. I had stopped enjoying it and was going through the motions, albeit still quite successfully.

CHAPTER TWENTY THREE
Pre Season sun and Cup agony

What was keeping me going was the new football season, and before that Dan and I had booked up to go to Cologne for a pre season tournament called the Colonia Cup where four teams play twice across the weekend. I had been to Cologne forty years earlier as a chorister with the choir of St Andrews Parish Church, Rugby. We sang in the imposing Cologne Cathedral which I remembered as an almost gothic monolithic building, the scale of which isn't easy to convey. Anyway, I was going again and after a good flight from Birmingham and train from Dusseldorf, we arrived in Cologne where immediately the Cathedral stands out at you. We found our hotel right behind the Cathedral and enjoyed a first glass of Kolsh, a very tasty local beer. From where we were sitting outside the hotel I was sure we could hear the strains of a Delilah, but couldn't quite place from where, so we went exploring.

We walked around the block by the very attractive river and having almost completed a circuit, we heard the sound get louder and found a couple of hundred Stoke fans holed up in four or five bars all adjacent to one another in the square, but centred on the Irish bar, The Corkonian.

We stayed for a while as an array of songs rang out and the locals seemed a bit stunned by this late afternoon sing song led by a couple of dozen lads who had clearly been at the bar for some time. There were a couple of vans of riot police nearby and while that initially looked quite intimidating, it was no more that precautionary and the evening went off without a hint of a problem. Dan and I were looking for a bite to eat and decided to venture a little further away from the merriment for our dinner where we enjoyed a fabulous steak. We decided to take in the atmosphere again before calling it a day and not long before midnight we adjourned for the night.

I owed Dan that trip, he didn't come with us to Valencia as it was his GCSE year and I was reluctant to take him out of school. On balance I regret that and so this opportunity to take in Cologne was too good to miss. I could tell he was enjoying it and at seventeen had a glass or two of cider.

The following morning was a glorious sunny day and after a hearty breakfast in the hotel we walked around the river and back toward the group of bars where most of the fans were set up. The array of flags and banners across the bars and on the fountains etc were a sight to behold and Dan was well pleased, so we spent a couple of hours in the sun, sipping a beer and chatting to various Stokies who were lapping it all up.

Getting to the match was one of the memorable parts of the trip. As the main groups of fans left the town for the tram, where travel was included in the match ticket, we crammed onto a coach of the tram and enjoyed it as it trundled toward the stadium and songs rang out all along the way. The other teams playing in the tournament were Koln, the hosts (who we were playing first) then Porto (who we were playing the following day) and lastly Valencia.

We arrived in the blazing sun, and walked across a large park to get to the impressive stadium and walked flights of steps to get to the large away seating area. We took our seats among around 1500 Stoke fans and the noise began. There was a healthy crowd and the deal was that an hour after the first game, Porto would be playing Valencia so we planned to stay for that game as well.

The game itself wasn't great, but it didn't matter a jot. We started okay but Koln looked like they were adapting better in the heat than us and took the lead. We got what we wished for in the second half with a goal from the still smiling Peter Odemwingie with a glancing header. Ultimately we lost 2 – 1 as Glen Johnson pulled out of a challenge and allowed their striker to score a late winner from close range.

We watched the first half of the Porto v Valencia game and were impressed with Porto. I don't remember seeing Imbula play, who we signed for a record £18m in the January transfer window in 2016. There were a couple of hundred Porto fans and hardly any Valencia fans so the large away following from England helped make the occasion at the tournament.

A quieter night was enjoyed and the bars in the same area were again busy, but a combination of the heat and the beer was taking its toll on many and after another glorious steak, Dan and I headed to our room.

The following morning was our last as we could only stay for one match as we were due to depart on a family holiday as soon as we got back. That meant we couldn't stay for our game against Porto, where we lost 3 – 0. On the short walk back to the railway station, we bumped into John Walters and Arnie in the square by the Cathedral, shook hands and had a brief chat. It rounded off a memorable trip that we were both eager to repeat!

We cashed in a few chips in the close season with the sales of Nzonzi to Seville for £8m, Begovic to Chelsea for £7m and Robert Huth to Leicester, where he had successfully been on loan and was pivotal in keeping them up the previous season, for £2m. With those funds Xherdan Shaqiri arrived for £12m, a record signing for the club and striker Joselu arrived for £5.75m and also the elegant Dutch

211

midfielder Afellay. Glen Johnson had arrived on a free and Marco Van Ginkel was also on loan. We felt the signings represented good business and in Shaqiri, the type of flair player who most Stoke fans thought we would never be able to attract.

We were still on holiday in Bruges on the opening match of our season against Liverpool and Dan and I found an Irish bar which was screening the game. A couple of fellow Stoke fans were also in the bar, and were as keen as us to register another famous victory, following our 6 – 1 win on final day of last season. It wasn't a great game with few chances and was settled by a crisp strike from Coutinho very late in the game.

We were back home for the Spurs game, our first away match and Dan and I headed off to White Hart Lane to clock up a new ground for him. Despite very loud vocal backing in the brilliant sunshine, things didn't look good when we conceded twice in the first half. Both goals were sloppy and at half time we had a mountain to climb. The Marc Muniesa song was fully utilized in the first half and was maintained for around twenty minutes. This even amused the locals. Jack Butland was in goal now and we had high hopes for him, a young talented English keeper who we stole from Birmingham for less than £3m.

It was stalemate for the first twenty minutes of the second half, but the introduction of Joselu and Stephen Ireland made a real difference. We looked livelier and had a couple of chances to get back in the game (which we missed) and feared that our moment had passed. However, Joselu was fouled in the box on 78 minutes and Arnie stepped up to score the resulting penalty and give us a chance. The decibels were rising and we were flowing forward as Spurs looked visibly nervous. Soon afterwards, Ireland crossed delightfully for Diouf to get the faintest touch on the ball and it slid into the corner for an equalizer that was greeted with wild celebrations.

Ireland almost scored himself soon after, but we were grateful for a hard earned point and a great comeback. We walked back to the railway station taking in the warm sunshine and had a drink with a few Spurs fans at Liverpool Street before heading home and looking forward to Match of The Day.

We lost against West Brom at home, our new bogey team since Tony was installed as manager and where both Adam and Afellay were sent off in the first half. Stoke still managed more than 50% possession! After also losing at Arsenal we went on a good run. First we drew at home to Leicester after being 2 – 0 up and rampant. Jamie Vardy conned the referee into giving a penalty as he has done many times since. No one gave a second thought to the possibility that we were playing the Champions elect. Then wins against Bournemouth (our first league victory), Villa and Swansea put us back on track.

The home win against Chelsea was memorable, a fine strong finish from Arnie who has become a real player acclimatized to the rigors of the Premier League. In the same month we won at Southampton through a Bojan penalty and then the game which really made me sit up and believe we were definitely on the verge of something special. We beat Man City 2 – 0. It wasn't the score line, the clean sheet etc it was the manner. It was a demolition similar to the Liverpool result and was so emphatic it took us a while to believe it had happened in the way it did. Just a shame Arnie didn't cap it with the hat trick he deserved, hitting the right upright after being put through.

All change at the Bank.

At the Bank more changes were being announced. I was invited to relocate to Manchester and continue looking after the network of regional offices. The way I was feeling about work meant it was an

213

easy decision to make and I declined that offer and instead left the bank after eight years, and the banking sector after thirty seven years.

I have no regrets, I largely enjoyed my career and things had changed so significantly I was happy to leave it behind. The environment had become one in which every decision was analysed by layers of committees, assembled on the pretense that they are protecting the Bank. It was governance gone mad.

I liken it to playing a match with a team who possess limited skill, little pace and almost no eye for goal. With those type of players, you can steal the odd draw but rarely win, and almost never, ever excite.

Credit, Risk and Audit functions had the upper hand. It was intended to protect the Bank, and sometimes it did. At the same time it stifled the truly gifted, creative members of the team who could really connect with customers and inspire memorable victories and results.

And now that pool of average players had hold of the ball, by god they weren't about to lose possession. It's like watching Alan Hudson and Jimmy Greenhoff dance their way through an opposition defence and lay the ball up on the six yard line ready to be tapped in. These business preventers could just smack the ball into an empty net instinctively, but instead always pause, take a touch or two and more often than not waste the fabulous opportunity created by the really skillful members of the team.

Anyway, we parted on good terms and I worked through to the end of April 2017 to enjoy a series of goodbyes and effect a handover. I had eventually escaped. I was relieved albeit a bit sorry for the colleagues I was leaving behind.

Back to the important stuff, we repeated the Man City performance and win over Man Utd, though this was more workmanlike and earned a comfortable 2 – 0 result. The control we were able to exercise was just stunning. The game of the season was next at Everton an absolutely thrilling 4 – 3 win with a last minute penalty coolly taken by Arnie (even though he slipped while taking it). I missed this game, when I go to Everton we get hammered!

It was a topsy turvy kind of season, and we would lose three in a row all 3 – 0, against Leicester away, Man Utd away and Everton at home. Then win three in a row at Bournemouth and at home to Villa and Newcastle.

The New Year brought some Cup interest and it was Dan's eighteenth birthday and he wanted to take some mates to see us play at Doncaster. I was thrilled when he said he wanted me to join as well and I organized a good trip, a few beers and an enjoyable game where we won 2 – 1 with great goals from Crouch and Walters. A great day out. Unfortunately Palace knocked us out in the next round in a meek performance. This was very disappointing as it was a competition we had high hopes in.

In the League Cup we had progressed at the expense of Luton and Fulham, both away from home. Then Chelsea and Sheffield Wednesday at home. Chelsea was the pick of the bunch. Dan, Tom and I were up for the game with the usual lads and it turned out to be a cracker. Begovic had returned to face us in goal for Chelsea. After a goalless first half where Chelsea had most of the possession, we took the lead through a neat turn and shot from Walters that went in off the underside of the crossbar. It looked for all the world that we would hold out for another famous win in the League Cup against Chelsea when Remy popped up to bury a flick on in the last minute. There was still time for Bardsley to be sent off and now we had to face thirty minutes of extra time with ten men.

Diouf, a striker, came on and played his heart out at right back and the bear pit atmosphere had returned to the Brit as every challenge and moment was cheered to encourage the lads to hold out. They did and it would be penalties, at the Boothen End. Begovic, who had celebrated the Chelsea equalizer a little too eagerly, was getting everything the crowd could (verbally) throw at him being reminded constantly of his diabolical record against penalties. All the first nine pens were top draw, and to be fair, Begovic got closer to ours than Butland had gotten to theirs. We scored our fifth penalty and then it was for Hazard to take the 10th spot kick. Hazard, one of the most lauded players in the world stepped up and cracked a shot high and hard but not leaving Butland for dead and he thrust up a hand to deflect the ball on to the bar. It was epic and we had won.

We got a kind home quarter finals draw against Championship Sheffield Wednesday and won through fairly comfortably 2 – 0. Next up were Liverpool again, this time over the two legged Semi-Final. In the home leg we didn't really do ourselves justice and they scored late in the first half and held on to that precious lead to take back to Anfield.

We had our tickets for the away leg and I was feeling surprisingly upbeat, Liverpool were not the force of old and we needed to take the game to them, without fear. We had to win at Anfield for the first time since 1959 to have any chance of making the final.

It was a rough journey to Liverpool and thank goodness for the sat-nav which directed us off the M6 and through a detour which was still busy but saved us a good hour and got us there with half an hour to go. One quick pint and a burger in the fan park and we were in. There was lots of confusion at all the entrances and the stewards were about as unhelpful as it's possible to be. I got separated from Dan and Garry who had travelled with me but we met eventually in our seats a few minutes before kick off. Many Stoke fans were delayed in the traffic. The policing was also a bit over the top. We were well into the first half when Ade and Max joined us and we noticed that Steve, Joe and Emma plus Simon and Rosco were already in the ground a few rows back.

It was noisy and with nervous hopefulness, we set about our business. We kept them quiet during the first half and created a few half chances but nothing clear cut until the forty fifth minute when Bojan got away down the wing and crossed for Arnie to score expertly at the near post. Replays suggested he was marginally offside, but we were in raptures and didn't care in the slightest. We had the equalizer in the tie now and just needed to cap the second half with a winner. Liverpool came more to life in the second period, but we looked the likelier to get the next goal and the desperate defending of Sahko, who is one of the worst centre halves I have seen in the Premier League, showed they were under pressure. Bojan was subbed and Charlie Adam came on, got some dreadful treatment from a few cynical Liverpool players who were not adequately penalized, and had to leave the field with an injury. Flanagan was the biggest, though not only Liverpool culprit. Later Arnie also left the pitch injured and while this brought Shaqiri on, he was more hesitant and showed great skill but not the drive that Arnie was delivering.

At full time we had won at Anfield for the first time in 56 years. But just 1 – 0 and so extra time, when some of the changes I have mentioned above took place. We did have one gilt edged chance to win it as Van Ginkel hit a post after being sent through from a 45 degree angle.

It went to penalties and for us three nailed on penalty takers were off the pitch, in Adam, Arnie and Bojan.

We went first at the away end and stood watching in fear and awe. Walters took our first kick and scored. They equalized. Crouch next, his shot saved, our heads went down. Emre Can misses for Liverpool and we were level again. Whelan scores and then Benteke scores with ease. Afellay scores our fourth and Firmino equalizes. Shaq next and a confident finish, 4 – 3. Milner keeps his head and its 4 – 4. Van Ginkel is next up, we are worried, he scores and we celebrate, we know its sudden death now and a miss puts us through. I have my arm around Dan's shoulder on the verge of Wembley. Lucas levels and his celebration confirms that he is the dick we all thought he was. Muniesa is up next and Mignolet who is generally a poor keeper but strong at penalties saves a powerful shot. If Liverpool score the next penalty it's all over. Joe Allen is taking it. Joe Allen who is now an established Stoke City player. We pray he misses. Allen coolly steps up, and scores. It is over and we are devastated. Lucas reconfirms what we all thought about him.

A long and quiet trip home after appreciating the herculean efforts of the lads. It kind of finished our season so much did it take it out of us and the injuries sustained.

Justice was done in the final. Liverpool should have been beaten by a cricket score by Man City, but found a break to equalize and took the game through extra time and to their best chance of winning; penalties. And who do you think misses the Liverpool penalty that gives the cup to Man City? Yep, Lucas. What goes around comes around son.

We only won two of our last ten matches. I was at both, and enjoyed the win at Watford, where we dominated and Joselu showed some class and poise to lob Gomes to make it 2 – 0. They got a consolation but it was never in doubt and a good away day to boot. We suffered some heavy defeats in those last group of games but were able to bounce back on the final day with an undeserved win

218

over West Ham, who were aiming for Europe. We recovered from a goal down when Imbula charged forward and scored from outside the box then in the dying moments Diouf scored a fabulous header to enable us to win the points. We held on to ninth place and finished above Chelsea in the Premier League.

CHAPTER TWENTY FOUR
The current season

Nearly up to date now, but a few more memories still to record.

Why can't we start a season strongly? We just keep stuffing it up. We had lost our first choice keeper and with Shay Given standing in, this weakness showed. We needed cover for goalkeeper, a centre half and a striker. Also, Imbula our record signing wasn't setting the world on fire and we needed more defensive midfield cover too.

It didn't happen straight away, but eventually we got all of the pieces we needed. Lee Grant and second choice at Derby joined as goalkeeper and has been a revelation. Joe Allen arrived and was a bargain for the role he undertakes, he still cost £12m. Bruno Martins Indi is exactly the centre half we had been looking for and in Ramadan Sobhi, I think we have unearthed a real talent who will feature prominently for us in the future. The strange one, which caused a lot of excitement at the time, was Wilfred Bony, the man mountain striker from Man City, but he has disappointed and can't make the team at all, especially as we have now completed the signing of Saido Berahino. I want Berahino to be the next Mark Stein, but I fear he is nowhere near that. Please god, let me be wrong!

What else changed? Well the ground has been renamed the Bet365 Stadium with the Coates family continuing to invest in the club. We are also finalizing the redevelopment to add seating in the corner of the Sharp Stand where away fans sit and the Family Stand. This will take the capacity to just over 30,000.

Pre-season didn't ignite the blue touch paper, but it gave Dan and I another opportunity to visit Germany. Hamburg this time. Hamburg is a quite different prospect to Cologne however, it's a massive city and in the North of Germany. Our previous experience gave us the confidence to go and we flew off and explored some of Hamburg on a chilly first evening before the game. We had a fairly early night and hoped for a good day to follow.

After breakfast we headed out, but immediately the heavens opened. Just ten minutes later the rain stopped and we were walking toward the city by the lake where we spotted a few Stoke fans. The weather continued to improve and we kept on walking toward St Pauli. We encountered the largest Gay Pride march ever and this entertained us for a while as an array of colourful sights drifted by. The sun was shining now.

The London Pub where a number of Stoke fans had assembled wasn't a great venue so we settled for a beer in an area nearby with some fabulous open air bars and music playing. We met a few Stoke fans and chatted about their experiences in Hamburg and the match to come.

We were in good spirits as we headed for the Metro and were befriended by a Hamburger Fan on the train who invited us to go with him and show us the best way to the ground. German folk are just so helpful, polite and friendly. Their English is almost perfect and they like beer. At the stop for the ground, after a short shuttle bus ride we alighted and made our way to our allocated part of the stadium. By now the sun had certainly got his hat on and we were about to enter a very impressive stadium indeed. There was a good crowd including around seven hundred Stoke fans on the lower tier where we were stood, yes stood, we were on the terracing and it was great! The game was a bit inconsequential, we were having a ball and they were serving beer and hot dogs.

We lost the match 1 – 0 and most fans stayed behind for a last hurrah and sing song, and waited for the players to come out for a warm down. The sing song became quite a bit more than that and turned into something epic, with the usual repertoire of songs then an edition of "Please don't take me home", which despite not being my favourite tune really caught on and the chorus rang out for fifteen or twenty minutes relentlessly.

By now we were almost the only ones left in the ground, save for a few dozen Hamburger fans, who were taking pictures and were very entertained if a bit confused. It continued, Charlie was in fits of laughter and came over and gave his top to one of the younger fans at the front, and still it continued. The number had dwindled to around 400 by now and they were hardcore, climbing every vantage point and many with shirts off continued the chanting.

I was due to meet Owen and Neil, who had been in the upper tier of the stand but had to text them to tell them that it was still jumping inside. They could hear all this on the outside but couldn't re-enter. My son loved every moment and when it was time to leave it was with broad smiles on every face, including many Hamburger fans who lined the path back to the Metro. They massively outnumbered the away fans clad in red and white, and amid scenes of mutual appreciation, we headed back to town for a quick beer before meeting again for dinner and then a late night as we discussed every aspect of our beloved club.

Fans generally remark that the atmosphere at the Bet365 for home games has declined, but at away games it's as good as ever with great belief in our ability to get results, or at least try to anyway.

Middlesboro away was the first destination of the new season and quite a few of the lads were keen to make the long trip. Dan and I were amongst them for a new ground for us both. I had been to Ayresome Park years earlier, but on a brilliant sunny day for their first game back in the Premier League, the Riverside looked good and was packed to the rafters. All was going so well until the game started! It wasn't that bad actually and we conceded a sloppy goal early on that didn't help, but Boro are pretty toothless and I figured we would have our own chances. Shay Given was the keeper as Butland was now on long term recovery after an ankle injury while playing for England and we desperately needed him back or another option.

In the second half we started to create a few more openings. From one of these, after Arnie was fouled near the left corner of the box, and was booked for dissent in the new supposed crackdown, Shaq lined up the free kick. From a seemingly impossible opening, he found the base of the far post and it was in. Great goal and celebration. Neither side went really close after that and we were probably glad of an honourable point to get the season underway.

After that things went Pete Tong, we lost four in a row and looked incredibly leaky at the back, enter Lee Grant and Bruno Martins Indi, both of whom made a big difference. The defeat at Palace, themselves a poor side who would be involved in the relegation mix, was utterly abysmal as we folded in the first half and even a late strike by Arnie from outside the box didn't add much cheer.

The turn of fortune came when we drew at Man Utd where Grant made some stunning saves to keep us in the game. They took the lead in the middle of the second half and while we kept pressing I wasn't very confident. However, after Walters chased a lost cause and the ball looped into the box, Crouch was right there waiting to pounce, but it struck the bar and bounced out over him. Luckily Joe Allen was also in the box and he gleefully stabbed the ball in and

223

celebrated his first goal and our first Premier League point at Old Trafford.

We won the next three games against lower half teams and faith was restored, although a growing undercurrent of discontent was becoming more visible, aimed directly at the Manager. Dan and I were looking forward to going to West Ham and their new London Stadium, where they had lost a few matches already. We were meeting up with Tony Peroni in the Bat and Ball in Westfield beforehand and Ade and his wife Sally. Steve and Emma also joined. The approach to the stadium was really impressive and while the seats are set back quite a way, the view is excellent. A good atmosphere in the ground and we played well, especially Sobhi in the first half giving us a glimpse of his talents. Despite having the bulk of the possession we conceded a soft deflected goal which I thought would excite the locals more than it appeared to. We kept our shape and pressed harder. Walters went on a run down the wing chasing a long ball and it took us a second or two to realize he was favourite to get there ahead of their keeper who was charging out of his goal. They clattered into each other, or more accurately Walters lifted the ball over him and he took Walters out. It would have been a penalty but the ball reached Bojan who had only just come on and he volleyed first time to equalize. It would be the final goal we would see the little maestro score for us before going out on loan. A well earned point.

More wins against lower half teams again took us to our established position of 9th where we have finished in all of the previous three seasons. Losses at Arsenal, then at both Liverpool and Chelsea followed. We scored in all these games taking the lead at Arsenal through a Charlie Adam penalty then at Liverpool through John Walters. But ended up losing all three quite heavily.

The win at Sunderland was comprehensive and at home to Man Utd we conceded very late to a Rooney special free kick to draw 1 – 1. Hopefully the last goal I will ever see him score in a Man Utd or, more importantly, an England shirt.

At home to Everton, who were in seventh place and playing well, we enjoyed a good game and a 1 – 1 draw in which Peter Crouch scored his hundredth Premier League goal. More than half of these goals were for Stoke and he will be remembered as a true Stokie. Well done Crouchy and we look forward to your Hundred Club slot on Sky.

Shortly after we shipped four goals at Spurs before half time and so after losing that game by such a margin meant that the trip to Man City, after a good home win against Middlesboro, represented another game against top opposition that could get messy. The line up was a bit different and our pattern of play allowed us to get forward while staying solid at the back. Grant hardly had a shot to save in the entire match and only one neat effort from David Silva caused nervousness. We had our own chances in the first half as Sobhi drove forward on a couple of occasions. But 0 – 0 was a great result against a Guardiola side who hadn't failed to score in their nineteen games at the Etihad Stadium this season, including Champions League fixtures.

As the season drew to a close, we had a dismal run of results that has increased pressure on the Manager. Safety in the Premier League is assured, however there are criticisms about several aspects of the team and selection choices of the Manager.

It was our last home game of the season, an opportunity for next seasons new kit to be showcased and for the players to perform their traditional lap of honour after the match. We were beaten by a

225

hungry Arsenal side 4 – 1 and while we rallied briefly after a header from Crouch made it 2 – 1, they were by far the stronger side.

I saw Arsenal on TV against Crystal Palace just a few weeks earlier and they were a shadow of the side that beat us in an attempt to qualify for Champions League again. Something they have now missed out on this year for the first time in over 20 years.

After the match the ground was almost empty. I stayed on, I always do to applaud the players, but it was in a bare stadium and while the players did their job, it must have felt pretty hollow.

Away at Southampton was our final game and Dan wanted to go so I organized tickets. On a beautiful Sunday we travelled to the coast and after a quick beer in the sunshine at a very friendly pub, we made our way into the ground. I had heard that tickets hadn't sold out, but it became very busy in the away end and the fans attended with the obvious intention of giving strong support to their team. This was great, the atmosphere was really positive in a party kind of way and we played really well.

Having missed some chances in the first half we kept on pressing in the second half. From a delightful cross from Cameron on the right, Crouch leapt higher than anyone and scored a very good header. The celebrations were joyous and lengthy. After that it was the Jack Butland show. He made several great stops and enabled us to secure a final day win at St Mary's.

It wasn't a great season, but its over now, our Premier League place secure and we rebuild for next season. Our pre-season calendar includes another Germany trip, this time to Leipzig and Dan and I are looking forward to another amazing experience abroad following Stoke City.

CHAPTER TWENTY FIVE
Managers

Lets begin with the Pulis versus Mark Hughes debate.

I must admit to being shocked when Tony was relieved of his duties. He had done a momentous job for us, securing promotion, keeping us in the Premier League, taking us to Wembley in the FA Cup Semi and Final and into Europe where we acquitted ourselves admirably.

My initial thoughts were that we were sacrificing safety in the Premier League for possibly just a few places of potential upside in the league. Upon reflection, I was wrong. The safety we had secured was based on a one dimensional approach, although Tony had added some wingers to the mix which gave the impression of attacking intent and was important in bringing us some success.

Away games were a real trial. The "you are leaving this dressing room with a point, don't come back without it" mentality was a hard watch, and while every point we scrapped for in the first few years in the Premier League was cheered vigorously, it never looked as if we could transition. At home we were very solid and with a passionate support, we dug out victories, were great at clinging on to what we had got. We inevitably were stronger against the teams in the bottom half of the league (our genuine competition), especially in those early Premier League years where we would have gladly signed up for 17th place before a ball was kicked during the season.

A positive example of our resilience and defensive qualities was away at Anfield in our first Premiership season. It was a hot

September day and while we were enormously excited about the prospect of playing our league matches against giants such as Liverpool, there was always a sense of foreboding that made me sick to my stomach. The feeling that its going to happen to us, it was just a question of when. On visiting Manchester United in the same season we started with a similar set of feelings, a passionate, noisy away following giving loads of stick to Ronaldo and Co and ultimately we received a right good hiding on the pitch. It ended 5 – 0 in a game where we were lucky to get nil. Ronaldo seemed to respond to the jibes and scored two stunning free kicks, but while all this was horrible, we were effectively put out of our misery early on and so it was all about when and not if we would lose.

At Chelsea in January 2009, it was the more typical eventual outcome. Not typical in many ways as we were in the game until the very last few kicks of the ball after Rory Delap had skipped past a few challenges and scored neatly after 60 minutes. The predictable Chelsea pressure did eventually pay off and after it was 1 – 1, even with very few moments left, it felt so inevitable that their winner would come and we would be bold losers away once again. The prophecy was proved correct when Lampard lashed home their winner in injury time.

At the Liverpool game, I feared that we might be on the end of a pelting. There was a large sell out away following giving the quiet Scousers all sorts of gip, but it was going to happen, we all knew it. Gerrard had a goal disallowed (for no particular reason) and we were under the cosh. We had held out until half time with almost no possession and that felt good, but we all still knew that the inevitable was on its way toward us, engine on and in a high gear. I dealt with the emotion of that by knowing that their goal, or more likely goals would come and that whatever the final score, we deserved our bravery award as the lads had been really putting their bodies on the line.

228

I think it was with about ten minutes remaining that I really started to get nervous. Could we, would we, be able to hold out and take a point home with us? It was torture. I dealt with it like a few others toward the back of the away terrace by taking off my shirt, waving it frantically and giving everything to see us hold on. I started not believing at all (just emotion management really) and finishing so incredibly proud of our heroes. I think that's where I really started to believe that maybe we could compete and scramble enough points to prolong our top flight adventure – I needn't have worried.

By the way, Anfield, all the mystique, awe, the passionate Kop and Gerry and the Pacemakers music creating a magical atmosphere is a load of cobblers. Anfield is a poor, old fashioned ground. The intense atmosphere stuff is a myth, the low roof on the away terrace means a restricted view if you are anywhere near the back and the You'll Never Walk Alone hype is merely a tannoy playing, rather than any significant effort by the fans. It's just a falsehood to believe its a cauldron there.

However, it's just not physically possible to grind out results like this at every away game. If we get caught early, there was almost no way back (although Stoke fans at Newcastle and Villa might argue with this as we charged back from 2 goal deficits to earn draws in both games).

So I wasn't sure that the transition, that the next step, was in fact possible for us. I was openly nervous about Mark Hughes who had some mixed experiences in his managerial roles (unlucky at Man City, underperforming at QPR). Would he be able to successfully change the pattern of our results where we had relied heavily on home performances to earn the points required to stay in the league? I was sceptical.

At a Real Estate lunch event I attended in Birmingham in June 2013, not long before Hughes was appointed, I was sat by the guest speaker, Dennis Turner, who as well as being UK Chief Economist for HSBC, was also Fulham's Club Historian. He delivered an interesting and quite funny review of UK Economics and like most of his peers, was miles off with his economic predictions. After he had relaxed with a couple of glasses of red wine and I of course disclosed my passion for Stoke City (which is an automatic compulsion of mine within the first 30 seconds of a conversation with someone new) he was keen to warn me of his view of Mark Hughes and referred to him as "damaged goods". Thus increasing my nervousness when Mark was ultimately appointed.

I read in early 2014 that Dennis had sadly passed away aged 67 without having had the chance to reconsider his opinion of Mark Hughes who (thus far) has enjoyed three consecutive 9th place finishes in the Premier League. It's not all plain sailing and now in 2017 the pressure is really on Hughes after a disappointing campaign and a 13th place finish.

After a relatively slow start and some interesting signings, Bojan included (what a player he looked) the evidence is there for all to see. He has already taken us to a place I never knew might exist for our club.

At my club we were verging on the "keeping us up isn't enough" point, with slightly reduced home crowds, smaller away support and a growing "marmite" view on Tony as our manager. I am sure we will see this develop and deepen at West Brom where he currently manages.

I want to finish on this topic by making it totally clear that Tony did stuff for us that maybe no one else could of achieved. The promotion to the Premier League and garnering of those precious points in the early Premier League years are priceless contributions. Even without the additions of FA Cup Semi and Final appearances at Wembley and some memorable trips in the Europa League, we should forever be thankful of what he did for us.

Thank you Tony, your contribution will never be forgotten. I tend to think we should have found him a job upstairs at the club because his managerial journey since leaving Stoke has seen him manage both Crystal Palace and West Brom – neither of whom we have beaten in any games we have played against them when Tony was in charge.

In terms of Palace it's understandable, kind of. He has done to us what we did to so many teams. The tougher one to take is West Brom, a local competitor with whom we have regularly battled and possess an excellent track record against. We could really do with the usual six points from West Brom so the sooner he falls out with them and ends up suing them (as he usually ends up doing), the better. Then we can return to normality and enjoy these games once again.

Prior to the Tony Pulis and Premier League years, we have witnessed a real mixed bag, and like the Forest Gump box of chocolates, "you never know what you are going to get".

I enjoyed the Boskamp season. He was a character in a game where there aren't many left. The writing was on the wall before he left at the end of the 2005/06 season signing off with a 5 - 1 win at Brighton (where my son Dan was the Stoke mascot at the Withdean stadium and where Adam Rooney scored a hat trick). I also saw my team win 4 - 1 at Ipswich that season with Sammy Bangoura scoring the pick of the goals with a great volley.

Before Boskamp, we were Icelandic with Gudjon Thordarson.

This was a strange and slightly surreal experience as a number of Icelandic internationals arrived at the club. Other than Brynjar Gunnarsson in Midfield, the performances from the others were a bit up and down. The keeper Kristinsson was a liability, Stefan Thordarson produced a wonder goal against Premier League Charlton in a 4 - 3 reverse, but little else.

Gudjon's son, Bjarni, was obviously skilful, looked slightly over-weight and while I will never forget his (deflected) goal in the Playoff final at Millennium Stadium against Brentford, he was never the real deal.

A mention for Steve Cotterill who was manager briefly after Gudjon left. You are and will always be a quitter. Whenever you return to this club, you will be booed. It doesn't matter if that's in 20 years time. And things like my book will remind our newer supporters of your treachery and deceit.

Prior to Gudjon, it was Tony's first spell at the club. If you look at the stats he did well enough and many were sorry to see him leave at that point. Not many (me included) were so keen on his return, at he time.

Going back, there are two more managers for me to comment on. Alan Ball is the first. World Cup winner and superhero midfielder. Let's get this out there straight away, Alan was no manager. He once famously managed 3 teams to relegation in a single season (some feat).

Apart from the odd and amazing occasion like the end of season 4 - 1 win at Brighton, after we were already down, there was little to cheer. That game was incredible, a huge following to the seaside on the open terrace at the old Goldstone ground all in beach wear and on the pitch after (in our case with a giant Pink Panther!)

Bally had to go and soon did the following season.

As I have covered earlier, I later met and made my peace with Alan on a trip to watch England play. Alan died in 2007 as he attempted to put out a fire in his back garden. RIP Bally.

Last, but by no means least, Lou Macari. A whole book could be attributed to Lou. He was magical for the club. He made astute signings and will forever remain a hero of mine. Lou secured the services of Mark Stein, TGO (the golden one) and Steino delivered. He followed up with the best piece of wheeling and dealing I have ever seen in football as he swapped Keith Scott for Mike Sheron – need I say anything more.

Lou took us to the Autoglass Trophy final at Wembley, which of course we won through a Steino cracker, though we would have preferred to be there a week later in the play off final, a game that Stockport had reached instead by knocking us out.

The following year he won the league title (Division 3). Steino scored 30 goals that year. He was the Messiah!

Lou left Stoke to become the manager of Celtic. Upon his departure, the then Celtic manager, Joe Jordan came the other way to Stoke. Joe was, in his time a battling and destructive striker. We hoped for a similar attacking approach. Instead he orchestrated a painfully slow and defensive oriented game. It wasn't good.

Lou returned to manage the club again and still plays a part in the local community in the Stoke on Trent area and has established a homeless centre for young adults in Hanley, The Macari Centre. Profits from this book are being dedicated to his Centre (a *minimum* £1 for every book sale).

We have had several other managers over the time I have been supporting Stoke City. Alan Durban of course who guided us back to the top flight in 1979, being one of them. Unfortunately, after a good spell with Stoke, Alan left to manage Sunderland.

Might we have progressed quicker, with more sustainability if we had retained our best managers? The truth is we will never know. My head and heart tells me yes, but would we still have scaled these current heights? Maybe some of it is fate.

One thing I do know, the pain, utter dejection and seemingly hopelessness of the situations we have found ourselves in, serve to heighten the pleasure of finding a way back. Then to witness the kind of performance against Manchester City at home in the 2015/16 season is an experience to be cherished forever.

Confused about managers and my favourites and least favourites over the years I conducted a survey among our group of twelve Stokies, the team regulars, and there were some very interesting results. I asked for everyone's top three favourite Managers and their least favourite one.

One fairly common thread was the depth of feelings about Steve Cotterill; the anger about what he did to our club hasn't gone away and in most people's lists, he remains Public Enemy Number One.

On the positive side, there is genuine recognition of what Tony Pulis did for our club but some of the lads see him as a split personality. One who has done so much for the club that we should all be eternally grateful for and, at the same time, the capacity to be stubborn irrationally difficult and unreasonable (his litigious background bearing testimony to that). So he actually appears on both the favourite and least favourite lists – of some of the same people! We witnessed how Tony, manager of West Brom, managed the Berahino saga. It seems that more and more people are coming round to this Jekyll and Hyde personality of his.

A regular favourite among our group was Lou Macari, largely due to the energy and drive he brought to our squad and the magical pieces of business he executed, at a time when there was little or no money available. We will forever remember both his spells at the club with great affection. In contrast to the Quitter Cotterrill, Lou left us for his beloved Celtic and when they came knocking it was unwelcome and horrible, but at the same time, understandable he would want to give that job a shot.

The lads and I fall into two distinct age groups, Ade, Simes, Steve C, T4 and I are all around mid 50's. The young ones, Dan, Tom, Rosco, Laura, Joe, Emma, Gina and Max are in the 16 to 25 age range so luckily for them, haven't seen all of the managerial merry go round that we have. Some of the lads liked Boskamp, some thought he was a bit of a joke. No one really mentions Gudjon Thordarson even though he did eventually get us out of the third tier of English football. Even Chris Kamara escapes critisism despite having statistically the worst managerial record over his eight games in charge.

As for Mark Hughes, there is a general view that he is the right man for the job and that his record of three consecutive ninth place finishes endorse him and the style of football and caliber of new players he has introduced to the club.

I like the players he has brought in and I believe we really do have the right man at the helm to take our beloved club to the next level. But you know football, by the time this book is published it's just as likely that we will have a new manager in charge!

CHAPTER TWENTY SIX
Statto

I have paid dearly for being a glory hunter, suffering 30 years of pain prior to Stoke City reaching the promised land of the Premier League.

My children, and particularly my sons can't be labeled as glory hunters. They were plucked from opportunities to play with their mates in the garden or at the park and were whisked off at a fairly young age on generally long journeys to watch Stoke City.

Statto isn't a nickname I have given myself and comes mainly from the lads I go to most matches with at Stoke. Steve C really started it and it springs from an ability to talk about many matches from several decades ago, naming scorers and events that most had forgotten about.

For some reason I started keeping records of the matches I attended. These records were pretty detailed and much (but certainly not all) of the information can be sourced through the internet these days.

For the first 313 Stoke City games I attended, between 28th January 1976 and 7th May 1995, I kept these records. The final game I did this was away at Luton Town, the last game of the 1994/95 season. In this game we won on a warm sunny afternoon 3 – 2. Paul Peschilido, Toddy Orlyggson and Keith Scott were on target. We finished 11th in the Second Division that year with 16 wins, 15 draws and 15 defeats.

Almost 20 years of stats, and looking back at them now as I am writing this chapter of the book, its all a bit scary.

The data I was keeping included the following:

Opponents
How I travelled to the game
Who went with me
Half Time Score
Full Time Score
Result
Date and League Status
Whether it was on TV or not
Home or Away
My assessment of our performance out of 10
Crowd
Day or Night match
Approximate number of away fans
My Stoke Man of the Match
What Competition the game was in
Scorers (both teams)
Comments (about anything memorable really)
If I got a programme

And more besides.

No wonder I stopped after 20 years, this was becoming a real bind and its visible from how untidy the book gets toward the end that the discipline that I had in the early days had gone. I think I was updating it after a few games had passed rather than after each one.

Do I wish I kept it up, partly yes, what great data I would possess to call on for this book, but I did have a life to lead as well and so I am calling it a good effort. My eldest son now possesses the book which includes all sorts of other data during those 20 years and truly confirms that I am nuts and, yes undeniably, Statto.

My mates at Stoke don't even know I have all this, I am expecting them to disown me now, but I guess I am useful on occasions as I can update them about particular facts from games in the past. An example that came up in a pre-match conversation over a beer was the home game against Barnsley on 30th October 1993.

This was an unusual match that ended 5 – 4. The only 5 – 4 result I can recall since I have been supporting Stoke City. In this game we were 3 – 2 behind at half time, and recovered to record a 5 – 4 victory. I was able to update the lads with both the scorers and the scoring pattern.

We had conceded twice in the opening seven minutes and then clawed back to 2 - 2 through two own goals. We conceded again before half time to go in at the break 3 – 2. In the second half goals from Vinny Overson, Martin Carruthers and Nigel Gleghorn gave us a 5 – 3 lead and despite conceding again toward the end, the match finished 5 – 4. The crowd was 14,674 and I estimated there were around 700 away fans. I gave a performance score of 6 out of 10.

Stuff like that really! And what on earth was I thinking awarding a rating of just 6 out of 10 for such an amazing game.

To summarise, of the 313 games that I kept these records for, we won 131 (42%) drew 92 and lost 90. Total goals for were 407 and conceded 330. At least the goal difference was positive (unlike what we are used to seeing over recent years) though most of these games were against lower league opposition.

My data collection days aren't completely over however as I write a match report for every game that each of my sons attend. I also maintain a summary of matches attended, grounds visited etc. Dan, my eldest son now 19 years old has been to 205 games, winning 78 of these (38%) and scoring 256 goals and conceding 237 in the process.

Dan's first game was away at Swindon Town on 3rd November 2001. He was nearly 4 years old and he was a fabulous omen as we ran out comfortable 3 – 0 winners with Brynjar Gunnarsson, Chris Iwelumo and James O'Connor on the score sheet. He was soon attending his first home game at the Brit, this time against Wycombe Wanderers. The crowd was 12,911 at this game and we went on to win 5 – 1, Brynjar Gunnarsson again on the score sheet with two this time. I realized I needed to get him to every game if we were going to get these kind of results!

Reality kicked in at Dan's fourth game at home to Port Vale where we lost 1 – 0.

After 78 games in the lower leagues, Dan eventually saw us promoted and he attended his first Premier League match against Aston Villa on 26th August 2008. As we know, this was a stunner of a game in front of a packed Britannia Stadium where we recorded our first win 3 – 2.

Dan is mad keen on Stoke City and now enjoys his away matches at least as much if not more than home games and he sometimes goes without me if, on occasion, I cant get to the match. He has now been to 42 grounds, winning at 14 of these. His records show that he has seen John Walters score more goals than any other Stoke player so far, with 25. Crouchy is close behind on 22.

The collection of hand written match reports is starting to get a bit out of hand, as the A4 match report is accompanied by the match day programme and ticket (where a separate ticket exists) and each is preserved in an individual plastic envelope.

For Tom, my youngest son who is 16 years old now, the same process applies. His first game was against Wimbledon at home on 16th August 2003, Tom was three at that time and through a very late goal by Wayne Thomas, we won 2 – 1. Carl Asaba got our opener. Tom's introduction to the Premier League was also at the Aston Villa match. He has been to 28 grounds so far.

Tom has clocked up 153 games now winning 57 of those (37%), drawing 47 and losing 49. He has seen 186 goals scored and 158 conceded and his top goal scorer is also John Walters on 23 with super hero Ricardo Fuller next with 12.

We all met Tony Pulis after the Leicester game that saw us promoted to the Premier League and as well as giving us a few autographs, fans were asking him about possible new signings to which Tony replied that he was sure there would be a few. Tom, who was eight at the time said to him "We don't want to do a Derby do we Tony?" which we all found hilarious, especially Tony. We were glad about Derby having such a horrendous year in the Premier League though as it relieved us of our record of the lowest points total achieved in a top flight season.

My daughter Sarah is less of a Stokie, though she has attended quite a few matches. Sarah has just finished her university course in Leeds. Her first game was against Wolves on 8th August 2004 where we again ran out 2 – 1 winners on her debut. On this occasion the scorers were Daryl Russell and Clive Clarke. Sarah has been to a number of matches since including the aborted attempt to see us play

Arsenal at the Emirates in January 2011. I had secured the banks box for the game and had guests lined up as well as my sons and Sarah.

We travelled down by train and were looking forward to a great day out. The boxes at the Emirates are fantastic facilities, great food and service and it is a real treat – they are hellishly expensive though.

On the way it started snowing, quite a novelty in London. As we approached Euston the snow got heavier and when we got off the tube at Highbury & Islington the snow was several inches thick. We hadn't got far when we learnt the match had been called off. Massive disappointment.

The match reports that I write have become quite a bit more than just facts from the game. I now personalize the notes so that these are like a collection of letters to my sons from their Dad. Maybe one day they might be interested in some of the memories and personal messages I have recorded. I will keep this going I think. Both lads are a part of our group who I will introduce in the next chapter.

As well as all this, I still keep records of the grounds I have attended. I like the idea of 3 types of "92 Club" (which is a Club for those who have attended a first team match at all 92 football league grounds across England and Wales). The three versions that I track are; firstly getting to visit all 92 current league grounds, secondly, to see my team Stoke City play at all of the 92, and then finally the hardest of all, to visit and see my team play and win at all 92. I doubt I will live long enough to get that third part done.

However in respect of the first two, I have made a good fist of this so far and have 90 grounds done while watching Stoke. The problem is that as teams fall out of the football league and new teams are promoted into it, it creates new grounds to visit as part of the 92. Also, as new stadia are developed, the old grounds fall away. Of my

90 grounds, I am down to 85 which are current stadia in the football leagues, of which we have won at 52. I have much work to do.

I hoped but never expected that my sons would be such regular visitors to matches with me, and this is something that I cherish and wouldn't change for the world.

CHAPTER TWENTY SEVEN
The Team

There have been a few changes to the team over the last thirty years, but fundamentally, the grandfathers (not quite literally, though its only a matter of time) are Ade, who I have introduced in our time at Barclays together, Simon (Bruce Grobbelaar look-a-like), Steve C and myself. Simon T4 is also part of the team who you read about showcasing his Spanish speaking and driving skills in Valencia.

Then the young ones, in other words the offspring. Starting with Ade, he has two members, Gina and Max, it really is like land of the giants in Ade's family with both comfortably checking in at 6ft+. Maybe that's how Max saved my goal bound effort on the beach in Valencia.

Simon adds two to the team, Ross (Rosco) and Laura, while Steve pitches in with Joe (tough tackler and a bit of a drink spiller) and Emma, who feels the cold a bit and can comfortably keep up in the drinking stakes. More recently, Emma's boyfriend John has become a regular, albeit with Derby County tendencies. The final two are my sons, the youngest elements of the unit, Dan and Tom who you have heard quite a bit about during the course of the book.

Don't get me wrong, the football is important but the getting together for pre-match routines is just as much of the fun and often quite a bit more. We usually perm ten or so out of twelve for each home match and join up for away days as well.

The celebrations that take place in Row 19, occupied by the grandfathers have diminished in terms of their animation and don't really resemble the rucks that used to take place on the old Boothen End. The younger ones, being a bit more agile throw themselves about a bit more and it all still means as much as ever.

I hope we keep going for many years to come and have the opportunity for multiple European journeys starting with the next pre-season episode to add to Cologne and Hamburg adventures, this time in Leipzig.

The club have confirmed they have frozen season ticket prices for the 2017/18 season for the 10th year in succession and it's a real statement of their connection with the people who support them. I know that it's a small part of the income these days with the vast majority coming from TV revenues, but that's not really the point. Many clubs focus on maximizing the income opportunity rather than rewarding loyal fans. The effect of holding these season ticket prices means Premier League football at affordable levels, the cheapest seats in the Premier League. The club have effectively been reducing the price each year if you allow for inflation. It's a gesture that is thoroughly appreciated. Added to that is free coach travel to all away Premier League fixtures.

Post season, which seems to get shorter and shorter, especially when you add in a couple of pre-season games, is a quieter time among the team of friends as everyone takes well earned holidays (always carefully timed to avoid new season fixtures which are announced in June). We all stay in touch about transfer news and speculation and having gone our separate ways for a few months return to precisely the same original team shape as though there had never been a break in-between. A bit like the Terminator in Terminator II who gets blitzed to all parts and then rediscovers its normal shape as though nothing had happened.

I love all that and its reliability and know that if ever push came to shove, I could (and from time to time have) been certain of their support. It works both ways, like any family unit I suppose and that's really what it has become. Something to cherish and continue.

The banter of course doesn't stop, sometimes masking the level of affection that exists within our unit. The words can sound cruel, but always with a touch of comedy. You know, like the day when the tray of drinks slips and one by one the ten or so pints topple leaving a pool of mixed beer and lager in the deep tray. Then after decanting into the glasses again, while a bit lumpy in places, is still consumed. Like holy communion, but with more bacteria. These moments are never forgotten and everyone has one or two special moments to their name.

How different would it be if we found ourselves out of the Premier League and back in the Championship or in an even lower tier, as we have been for many of the years I have been following the club? I guess we will find out one day (not for a long time I hope) and my guess is that we will all turn up at the same time and in the same place, we will find parking easier and traffic generally lighter. There wont be the same queues for half time Bovrils and a pee break will involve less time too.

We will get tickets far easier than at present where its often necessary to book on line at that one minute past midnight to secure the tickets we need for West Brom away and many other fixtures. They will probably be cheaper too.

But the match day ritual wont change, its what we do and who we are. And we most definitely know who and what we are, we are Stoke City, the pride of the Midlands.

CHAPTER TWENTY EIGHT
The End, or just the beginning?

Stoke City's roots span back to 1863, almost one hundred years before I was born. I have been lucky enough to have seen my club enjoy great years, back at the start of the 1970's and during the last decade where, arguably, the club have achieved more success than at any point in its 150 year history.

If you had asked me ten years ago everything I could have (realistically) hoped for from my team and had offered me promotion to the Premier League, sustained performance in that division for a decade, an FA Cup Final and a European adventure, I may have laughed at you. It would certainly have been everything and more than I could have wished for from the club.

Now of course, we have done all that, the crowd has got used to the team improving year on year in terms of their personnel and achieving a hat trick of ninth place finishes. The same intense atmosphere doesn't always exist at the Bet 365 Stadium, though it sometimes returns against the likes of Arsenal and Man Utd. Do we take for granted our existence in the Premier League? Maybe we do, maybe I do, and perhaps only the shock of potentially dropping out of our sublime surroundings will be the catalyst for a return of the Bear Pit, to ensure we gain those priceless points each year.

The talent on the pitch has never been richer (literally!) though the blend of players and the chemistry is a hard cocktail to mix and manage.

So if you were to ask me again, what realistically is everything I would wish for from my team if I am lucky enough to be around to enjoy the next ten years. Well, for me it wouldn't be much more than we have had. I would ask for continued Premier League status. I would ask for another Cup Final, and a win this time and one more European adventure to savour. Is that asking too much? We were a hairs breadth from a League Cup Final appearance last year after that cruel night at Anfield and with just a little bit more care and attention, especially against lower league opposition, I think the passage is possible.

But lets be greedy, if you asked me again in 2027 after another decade had passed, who knows, maybe I would be chomping at the bit for Champions League and possibly a challenge for the league title. But I doubt it. What I wish for more than all this is the opportunity to continue my journey supporting the club, with my team of mates at Stoke, with Ade, Steve, Simes, T4, Rosco, Emma, Joe, Max, Laura, Gina and my sons, Dan and Tom.

Nothing remains constant. I never imagined for years that I would ever see my team's home other than at the Victoria ground. And now we have been at the Brit and (now the Bet365) for 20 years I can't imagine a time when they will be anywhere else. But they will, just as all of the players, managers, and supporters will pass away and new generations will pick up the gauntlet.

Will they remember our current Premier League stars, Arnie, Crouchy, Ryan, Joe Allen and many others. Will the memory of Matthews, Banks, Greenhoff, Hudson, Steino, Ricky and all our great players and heroes over the decades, representing our club with honour, live on forever? I hope so, they deserve it.

As I finish this book, some friends have been asking me if I will write another. I don't know. Maybe that depends on what you all think of this attempt to capture some memories over the last forty years, spanning five decades.

Others enquire if it's all been worth it. The cost, thousands of miles travelling and the pain and heartache endured along the way. In short, *Was the juice really worth the squeeze?* It's a simple answer.

It has always and will forever be worth it

I said it was emotional and it is for me.

We love you City, we do.